IMAGERY

John T.E. Richardson
Brunel University, UK

Psychology Press
Taylor & Francis Group
HOVE AND NEW YORK

Transferred to Digital Printing 2010

Psychology Press
27 Church Road
Hove
East Sussex, BN3 2FA
UK

Psychology Press is a members of the Taylor & Francis Group; an informa business

British Library Cataloguing in Publication Data

A catalogue record for this book is available from the British Library
ISBN 978-0-86377-843-8 (pbk)

ISSN 1368–4558 (Cognitive Psychology: A Modular Course)

Cover design by Joyce Chester
Typeset by Mendip Communications Ltd, Frome, Somerset

Contents

Series Preface

Cognitive Psychology: A Modular Course, edited by Gerry Altmann and Susan E. Gathercole, aims to provide undergraduates with stimulating, readable, affordable brief texts by leading experts. Together with three other modular series, these texts will cover all the major topics studied at undergraduate level in psychology. The companion series are: Clinical Psychology, edited by Chris Brewin; Developmental Psychology, edited by Peter Bryant and George Butterworth; Social Psychology, edited by Miles Hewstone. The series will appeal to those who want to go deeper into the subject than the traditional textbook will allow, and base their examination answers, research, projects, assignments, or practical decisions on a clearer and more rounded appreciation of the research evidence.

Acknowledgements

This book was written whilst I was on study leave from Brunel University and working as a Visiting Research Professor in the Institute of Educational Technology at the Open University. I am very grateful to both these institutions for their support. I am also grateful to Michel Denis, Tore Helstrup, Bob Logie, Gerry Quinn, and Taeko Wydell for their comments on the draft manuscript of this book, to Michael Wright for his advice, to Emmanuel Mellet for kindly providing the cover illustration, and to Mark Mower for his assistance in preparing the figures.

John T.E. Richardson
March 1998

Cover illustration

The cover illustration shows single-subject normalised regional cerebral blood-flow (NrCBF) activation images superimposed upon the corresponding axial slice obtained from magnetic resonance imaging. The slices pass through the parietal (top panels) and superior occipital areas (bottom panels). Activation maps were obtained by subtracting the averaged NrCBF images in a control condition from the average NrCBF images obtained during visual perception (left-hand panels) or imagery (right-hand panels). In each image, the right hemisphere is shown on the left, and vice versa; increased activation is represented by colours towards the red end of the spectrum. In this participant, the occipital activation under both perception and imagery is accompanied by a parietal activation.

Note. From "A Positron Emission Tomography Study of Visual and Mental Spatial Exploration", by E. Mellet, N. Tzourio, M. Denis, and B. Mazoyer, 1995, *Journal of Cognitive Neuroscience*, 7, 441. Copyright 1995 by Massachusetts Institute of Technology. Reprinted with permission.

Introduction 1

> Image. . . . A mental representation of something (esp. a visible object), not by direct perception, but by memory or imagination; a mental picture or impression; an idea, conception. . . .
>
> *(Oxford English Dictionary)*

This contribution to a modular textbook on *Cognitive Psychology* has to do with the concept of mental imagery. Investigations of mental imagery can be traced back over more than 2500 years, they were an important part of the earliest attempt to devise a scientific psychology in the 19th century, and they were at the forefront of the initial development of cognitive psychology in the 1960s. Since then, research on mental imagery has presented a challenge for mainstream cognitive psychology by generating new kinds of theory concerning potential mental representations and new methods for investigating those representations.

Conceptualising imagery

Research into imagery does not constitute a single homogeneous field, even within cognitive psychology, and it is all the more interesting as a result. However, this also makes it much more difficult for the outsider or the student to appreciate the different strands and how they hang together. I have found it helpful to classify research on imagery under four headings, and these provide the organising structure for the chapters in this book. One approach, perhaps the one that makes most sense to non-psychologists, is to focus upon imagery as a personal or phenomenal experience. A second approach, perhaps the one that makes most sense to other psychologists, is to focus on imagery as a mental or "internal" representation. A third approach, one which was represented in the earliest attempts to investigate imagery within cognitive psychology, is to focus upon imagery as a property or attribute of the materials that subjects have to deal with in laboratory experiments. The fourth approach, which figures prominently in recent research but originated in the earliest discourse concerning mental imagery, is to focus upon imagery as a process that is under strategic control.

Investigating imagery

Accordingly, in the chapters that follow, I shall try to present a coherent view of the relevant literature by dealing successively with these four ways of conceptualising imagery. Before doing so, however, I also need to explain that, within the paradigms and methods of cognitive psychology, imagery can be investigated in two different ways:

- as a dependent variable (in other words, as something that is *measured* by researchers), or
- as an independent variable (in other words, as something that is *manipulated* by researchers).

These two approaches are intrinsically complementary to each other, but they are inevitably associated with different kinds of research methodology.

Research in the first tradition has usually been concerned with the subjective and qualitative aspects of imagery (for example, its vividness or its controllability), and the extent to which mental images are structurally similar to the physical objects that are being imaged. These questions will be considered in Chapter 2. Research of this sort also considers the role of imagery as a strategy in remembering and in other cognitive tasks, and this issue will be discussed in Chapter 5. What is of interest under this heading is how the experience of imagery and the use of imagery vary from one person to another, from one task to another, or from one situation to another.

Research in the second tradition is, in many ways, more in keeping with the positivist, behaviourist, and experimentalist legacy that is still very much alive in contemporary cognitive psychology. Such research has usually been concerned with the objective, observable, and quantifiable aspects of cognition, which are reflected (it is hoped) in behaviour and especially in performance in remembering and other cognitive tasks. What is of interest under this heading is how observable performance is affected by variations in the abilities of the subjects, in the image-evoking properties of the experimental materials, and by the administration of instructions and other manipulations. These different questions will be discussed in Chapters 3, 4, and 5, respectively.

Imagery and the brain

Regardless of how imagery is investigated or conceptualised, all cognitive psychologists would nowadays agree that people's ability to create, contemplate, and manipulate images depends upon the integrity of structures, mechanisms, and processes in our brains. It is therefore interesting and important to try to understand the ways in which these structures, mechanisms, and processes mediate our subjective experience and observable behaviour. This will be an important part of the discussion in each of the four main chapters in this book, and accordingly it will be useful to summarise the main anatomical features of the brain to which I shall refer during these discussions.

Figure 1.1 shows a simplified view of the left side of the human brain. The cerebrum consists of two hemispheres that are connected by the three cerebral commissures, of which the most important is the great commissure or corpus callosum. Each of the two hemispheres consists of an inner core of white matter, surrounded by a covering of grey matter (the cerebral cortex). The cortex of each cerebral hemisphere is described in terms of four regions: the frontal lobe, the temporal lobe, the parietal lobe, and the occipital lobe. Areas within each of these lobes are identified by reference to different directions:

- anterior (to the front) versus posterior (to the rear);
- superior (above) versus inferior (below).

In humans and other upright species, "anterior" means the same as "ventral" (literally, "towards the belly"), and "posterior" means the same as "dorsal" (literally, "towards the back").

In this book, I shall consider three different kinds of evidence that help to elucidate the brain mechanisms involved in imagery. One kind of evidence is obtained by studying the behaviour of "normal" (i.e. intact) individuals. The classic contribution of what might be referred to as "experimental neuropsychology" has been the development of ideas about the representation of language in the human brain on the basis of procedures that permit the presentation of individual stimuli solely to one cerebral hemisphere. For example,

FIG. 1.1.
Exterior view of the
left side of the
brain. From *Brain
Damage, Behaviour,
and the Mind* (p. 4),
by M. Williams,
1979, Chichester,
UK: Wiley.
Copyright © 1979
by John Wiley &
Sons Ltd. Reprinted
with permission.

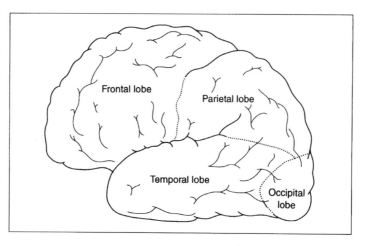

it is well known that when pairs of stimuli are presented simultaneously to the left and the right halves of the visual field (or to the left and right ears), recognition of the stimulus presented to the right visual hemifield (or to the right ear) is better if the items in question are verbal. Conversely, the recognition of the stimulus presented to the left visual hemifield (or to the left ear) is better if the items in question are difficult to describe or label in purely verbal terms. Given that, under these experimental conditions, each visual hemifield and each ear enjoy privileged access to the *opposite* hemisphere of the brain, these results are generally taken to confirm the view that the left and right hemispheres have different roles in the processing of verbal and non-verbal information.

In practice, however, these experimental methods involving lateralised presentations provide only weak evidence concerning the neural representation of psychological functions in the two cerebral hemispheres. A second approach is to obtain "on-line" recording of brain activity whilst the individuals in question are performing specific experimental tasks. This traditionally involved the measurement of changes in the electrical potential of the brain using electrodes attached to the scalp. The sort of record that is produced is known as an electroencephalogram (EEG). Researchers are sometimes interested in the specific changes in electrical potential that are evoked by presentation of a particular stimulus, and these are known as event-related potentials (ERPs). EEG and the newer but closely related technique of magnetoencephalography (MEG), which measures the magnetic field generated by the brain's electrical activity, provide a good account of changes over time, but the spatial views of the brain and its workings in cognitive tasks that are provided by these methods are relatively fuzzy and obscure.

The introduction of computerised tomography (CT) and especially magnetic resonance imaging (MRI) provided views of the brain which were of much higher resolution but which were intrinsically static in nature. Studies of regional cerebral blood flow using positron emission tomography (PET) provide a better view of brain activity during ongoing cognitive tasks, but these are less adequate in terms of spatial resolution. Accordingly, the state of the art in brain imaging research is to link these two approaches, thus exploiting their respective strengths, and research laboratories and clinical facilities around the world are adopting MRI and PET technology to study activity within specific brain structures over the course of time. In principle, these techniques can be used with both intact individuals and neurological patients, but for research purposes the subjects are usually normal volunteers.

A third approach is that of clinical neuropsychology: in other words, the investigation of psychological functions and processes in patients who have suffered actual physical damage to the central nervous system. These patients fall into three main categories. First, there are cases that result from physical injury to the head. In wartime, traumatic damage is associated with open wounds that are produced by weapons or shrapnel. In peacetime, however, such damage more often takes the form of "closed" head injuries in which the contents of the skull are not exposed. Second, brain dysfunction is also associated with neurological diseases, especially those of a histopathological nature (such as cerebral tumours) and those involving the cerebrovascular system. Third, brain damage may also arise as the consequence of surgical treatment intended to alleviate the symptoms of neurological disease.

Under the latter heading, two groups will be of particular interest in this book. Patients in both groups have typically undergone surgical treatment to alleviate chronic, intractable epileptic conditions. One group consists of patients who have undergone surgical resection of (a portion of) a temporal lobe. Bilateral temporal lobectomy (removal of *both* temporal lobes) is known to give rise to a severe amnesic condition, and most patients will have undergone a unilateral temporal lobectomy. The second group contains patients in whom the hemispheres have been separated by sectioning of the corpus callosum and perhaps the optic chiasm and the other commissures, too. This surgical procedure is described clinically as a commissurotomy, but it is more colloquially known as the "split-brain" technique.

Is imagery a right-hemisphere function?

The findings of research into the effects of brain damage tend to fit well with the experimental data from normal individuals mentioned earlier with regard to the relative contributions of the two cerebral hemispheres to performance in linguistic and non-linguistic tasks. For example, patients who have lesions of the left temporal lobe are found to be impaired in tests of verbal memory but not in tests involving complex displays that cannot be readily described or labelled, such as unfamiliar human faces or abstract pictures. Conversely, patients who have lesions of the right temporal lobe are generally found to be impaired in the latter tests of non-verbal memory, but not in tests of verbal memory (see, for example, Milner, 1971).

Mental imagery can of course be used to represent verbally presented information, but it is not tied to a specific way of expressing that information. It can also be used to represent events and experiences that are difficult to label or describe. Hence, mental imagery appears to be an intrinsically non-verbal mode of thinking, and one might therefore anticipate that the neuroanatomical basis of mental imagery would be contained in the right cerebral hemisphere. In fact, this idea has quite a long history. Ley (1983) quoted the English neurologist Hughlings Jackson as writing over 100 years previously that "the posterior lobe on the right side [of the brain] . . . is the chief seat of the revival of images" (p. 252). Nowadays, the general idea that the right cerebral hemisphere is somehow specialised for mental imagery pervades a good deal of popular writing. Nevertheless, as Ehrlichman and Barrett (1983) pointed out, this idea needs to be evaluated critically and carefully against possible alternative hypotheses.

One assumption underlying this idea is certainly unlikely to stand this test. This is the idea that imagery is based upon a single mechanism that is localised within just one cerebral hemisphere. Kosslyn (1980) put forward the idea that imagery depends upon a complex system which consists of a large number of different components or subsystems. This idea is generally accepted, even though researchers may disagree over what these components actually are. Consequently, it is the localisation of these different components within the brain (and especially their lateralisation between the two hemispheres) that needs to be addressed by neuropsychological research, and, accordingly, this will be a key theme in each of the chapters in this book.

Summary: Introduction

1. Researchers have conceptualised mental imagery in different ways: as a phenomenal experience, as an internal representation, as a stimulus attribute, and as a cognitive strategy.
2. Imagery can be investigated either as a dependent variable or as an independent variable. The two approaches are complementary but involve different kinds of research methodology.
3. Imagery depends on the integrity of structures in the brain. These can be investigated by using the methods of experimental neuropsychology, by using physiological recording and brain-mapping methods, and by studying the effects of brain damage.
4. It is widely assumed that imagery is based upon a single mechanism that is localised in the right cerebral hemisphere. This idea that imagery is a right-hemisphere function needs to be critically examined. The idea that imagery is based upon a unitary mechanism is certainly open to question.

Imagery as a phenomenal experience 2

Mental imagery is essentially a "private" or "subjective" experience, in the sense that we cannot directly observe other people's mental images. This is equally true of other mental events, such as sensations, thoughts, and feelings. Instead, we get to know about other people's mental states on the basis of what they say and what they do. Sometimes, as in the case of pain or happiness, for instance, there is a characteristic way that a mental state is displayed in a person's behaviour: we can tell that somebody has toothache from the way that they hold their jaw and moan. Equally, however, we can tell that somebody has toothache because they say, "I've got toothache" (Wittgenstein, 1958, p. 24). In both cases, of course, they might just be pretending to have toothache, but this does not detract from the fact that we normally do come to know about other people's mental experience on the basis of their verbal and non-verbal behaviour.

In the case of some mental events, however, there does not appear to be any characteristic behaviour of this sort, and this seems to be true, in particular, of mental imagery. As Quinton (1973, p. 328) pointed out, there is simply no natural expression that corresponds to having an image of Salisbury cathedral. To be sure, there are certain behavioural signs that one might well observe while somebody was having mental image of Salisbury cathedral: they might have a thoughtful expression on their face, and they might be gazing towards a rather vague and unimportant area of space. But these signs would not distinguish between mental imagery and more abstract forms of thinking, nor would they tell us anything about the content of the person's mental images. As a result, we cannot come to know about other people's images on the basis of their observable non-verbal behaviour. Instead, we have to depend upon their verbal behaviour: in other words, upon what they say, rather than upon what they do. Accordingly, scientific research into mental imagery began with attempts to collect systematic verbal accounts of people's phenomenal experience.

Galton's "breakfast-table questionnaire"

The earliest research of this sort was carried out by Galton (1880; see also 1883, pp. 83–114), who devised a questionnaire in which respondents were asked to describe the quality of the mental imagery that was elicited when they tried to visualise familiar objects or scenes. The complete questionnaire is shown in Box 2.1. Although this instrument is often referred to as Galton's "breakfast-table questionnaire", the breakfast table was suggested merely as an example, and the respondents were essentially being invited to think of any specific object or scene. Most of the questions are explicitly concerned with visual imagery, although Question 12 asks the respondents to describe their imagery in other sense modalities, and Question 13 refers to imagery for music. Finally, unlike most modern questionnaires, Galton's instrument left the respondents free to describe their mental experience in their own words.

Galton began by approaching his friends in the scientific community, in the belief that they were the sort of people who would be most likely to give accurate responses:

> To my astonishment, I found that the great majority of the men of science to whom I first applied, protested that mental imagery was unknown to them, and they looked on me as fanciful and fantastic in supposing that the words "mental imagery" really expressed what I believed everybody supposed them to mean. (p. 302)

Galton inferred from this that "scientific men as a class have feeble powers of visual representation", and this he explained by proposing that "an over-readiness to perceive clear mental pictures is antagonistic to the acquirement of habits of highly generalised and abstract thought" (p. 304).

However, when Galton approached a wider cross-section of people whom he met "in general society", he obtained quite different accounts:

> Many men and a yet larger number of women, and many boys and girls, declared that they habitually saw mental imagery, and that it was perfectly distinct to them and full of colour. The more I pressed and cross-questioned them, professing myself incredulous, the more obvious was the truth of their first assertions. (pp. 302–303)

The object of these Questions is to elicit the degree in which different persons possess the power of seeing images in their mind's eye, and of reviving past sensations.

From inquiries I have already made, it appears that remarkable variations exist both in the strength and in the quality of these faculties, and it is highly probable that a statistical inquiry into them will throw light upon more than one psychological problem.

Before addressing yourself to any of the Questions below, think of some definite object—suppose it is your breakfast-table as you sat down to it this morning—and consider carefully the picture that rises before your mind's eye.

1. *Illumination.* Is the image dim or fairly clear? Is its brightness comparable to that of the actual scene?
2. *Definition.* Are all the objects pretty well defined at the same time, or is the place of sharpest definition at any one moment more contracted than it is in a real scene?
3. *Colouring.* Are the colours of the china, of the toast, breadcrust, mustard, meat, parsley, or whatever may have been on the table, quite distinct and natural?
4. *Extent of the field of view.* Call up the image of some panoramic view (the walls of your room might suffice), can you force yourself to see mentally a wider range of it than could be taken in by any single glance of the eyes? Can you mentally see more than three faces of a die, or more than one hemisphere of a globe at the same instant of time?
5. *Distance of images.* Where do mental images appear to be situated? Within the head, within the eye-ball, just in front of the eyes, or at a distance corresponding to reality? Can you project an image upon a piece of paper?
6. *Command over images.* Can you retain a mental picture steadily before the eyes? When you do so, does it grow brighter or dimmer? When the act of retaining it becomes wearisome, in what part of the head or eye-ball is the fatigue felt?
7. *Persons.* Can you recall with distinctness the features of all near relations and many other persons? Can you at will cause your mental image of any or most of them to sit, stand, or turn slowly around? Can you deliberately seat the image of a well-known person in a chair and see it with enough distinctness to enable you to sketch it leisurely (supposing yourself able to draw)?
8. *Scenery.* Do you preserve the recollection of scenery with much precision of detail, and do you find pleasure in dwelling on it? Can you easily form mental pictures from the descriptions of scenery that are so frequently met with in novels and books of travel?
9. *Comparison with reality.* What difference do you perceive between a very vivid mental picture called up in the dark, and a real scene? Have you ever mistaken a mental image for a reality when in health and wide awake?
10. *Numerals and dates.* Are these invariably associated in your mind with any peculiar mental imagery, whether of written or printed figures, diagrams, or colours? If so, explain fully, and say if you can account for the association?
11. *Specialities.* If you happen to have special aptitudes for mechanics, mathematics (either geometry of three dimensions or pure analysis), mental arithmetic, or chess-playing blindfold, please explain fully how far your processes depend on the use of visual images, and how far otherwise?
12. Call up before your imagination the objects specified in the six following paragraphs, numbered A to F, and consider carefully whether your mental representation of them generally is in each group very faint, faint, fair, good, or vivid and comparable to the actual sensation:
    a) *Light and colour.* An evenly clouded sky (omitting all landscape), first bright, then gloomy. A thick surrounding haze, first white, then successively blue, yellow, green, and red.
    b) *Sound.* The beat of rain against the window panes, the crack of a whip, a church bell, the hum of bees, the whistle of a railway, the clinking of tea-spoons and saucers, the slam of a door.
    c) *Smells.* Tar, roses, an oil-lamp blown out, hay, violets, a fur coat, gas, tobacco.
    d) *Tastes.* Salt, sugar, lemon juice, raisins, chocolate, currant jelly.
    e) *Touch.* Velvet, silk, soap, gum, dough, a crisp dead leaf, the prick of a pin.
    f) *Other sensations.* Heat, hunger, cold, thirst, fatigue, fever, drowsiness, a bad cold.
13. *Music.* Have you any aptitude for mentally recalling music, or for imagining it?
14. *At different ages.* Do you recollect what your powers of visualising, etc., were in childhood? Have they varied much within your recollection?

General remarks. Supplementary information written here, or on a separate piece of paper, will be acceptable.

Box 2.1. Questions on visualising and other allied faculties. From *Inquiries into Human Faculty and Its Development* (pp. 378–380), by F. Galton, 1883, London: Macmillan.

1. "Brilliant, distinct, never blotchy."
6. "The image once seen is perfectly clear and bright."
12. "I can see my breakfast table or any equally familiar thing with my mind's eye quite as well in all particulars as I can do if the reality is before me."
25. "Fairly clear; illumination of actual scene is fairly represented. Well defined. Parts do not obtrude themselves, but attention has to be directed to different points in succession to call up the whole."
50. "Fairly clear. Brightness probably at least from one-half to two-thirds of the original. Definition varies very much, one or two objects being much more distinct than the others, but the latter come out clearly if attention be paid to them."
75. "Dim, certainly not comparable to the actual scene. I have to think separately of the several things on the table to bring them clearly before the mind's eye, and when I think of some things the others fade away in confusion."
88. "Dim and not comparable in brightness to the real scene. Badly defined with blotches of light; very incomplete; very little of one object is seen at one time."
94. "I am very rarely able to recall any object whatever with any sort of distinctness. Very occasionally an object or image will recall itself, but even then it is more like a generalised image than an individual one. I seem to be almost destitute of visualising power as under control."
100. "My powers are zero. To my consciousness there is almost no association of memory with objective visual impressions. I recollect the table, but do not see it."

Box 2.2. Vividness of imagery in rank-ordered examples from 100 men. Quotations taken from "Statistics of mental imagery", by F. Galton, 1880, *Mind, 5*, 310–312. Reprinted by permission of Oxford University Press.

Galton concluded that there was considerable diversity in the experience of mental imagery among the general population.

He then set about obtaining responses from a larger sample of 100 of his male acquaintances, of whom a majority were "distinguished in science or in other fields of intellectual work" (p. 304). He found that he could order their responses to the first two questions (concerning illumination and definition) in terms of the vividness of their reported imagery, and Box 2.2 illustrates the range of responses obtained in this rank-ordering. Galton described a similar distribution of responses which he had obtained from a total of 172 boys taking science classes at the Charterhouse School in London. He also concluded from his investigations that "the power of visualising is higher in the female sex than in the male" (Galton, 1883, p. 99), but the results that he actually published were based solely upon the responses of men and boys to his questionnaire.

Betts's Questionnaire upon Mental Imagery

The first quantitative instrument for evaluating experienced mental imagery was developed by Betts (1909) on the basis of Galton's original questionnaire. He described it simply as a "Questionnaire upon Mental Imagery" (QMI), and it consisted of 150 items covering seven different sensory modalities.

The first section contained 40 items on visual imagery: eight about "your breakfast table as you sat down to it this morning", eight about "some relative or friend whom you frequently see", eight about "some familiar landscape which you have recently seen", eight about a short piece of lurid prose describing a murder scene, and eight miscellaneous items. The second section contained 20 questions on auditory imagery: four about a lecturer's voice, four about a familiar tune, and 12 miscellaneous items. The remaining sections contained 20 items on cutaneous imagery (feeling or touching different objects), 20 items on kinaesthetic imagery (performing different acts), 20 items on gustatory imagery (tasting different kinds of food and drink), 20 items on olfactory imagery (smelling different odours), and 10 items on organic imagery (feeling different bodily sensations).

For instance, the respondents were asked to think of

- the sight of the sun as it is sinking below the horizon;
- the sound of the mewing of a cat;
- the feeling of the prick of a pin;
- the feeling of running upstairs;
- the taste of salt;
- the smell of fresh paint;
- the sensation of fatigue.

In each case, the respondents were asked to use the following standard scale to judge the vividness of the mental images that were evoked (pp. 20–21):

1. Perfectly clear and as vivid as the actual experience.
2. Very clear and comparable in vividness to the actual experience.
3 Moderately clear and vivid.
4. Not clear or vivid but recognisable.
5. Vague and dim.
6. So vague and dim as to be hardly discernible.
7. No image present at all, you only *knowing* that you are thinking of the object.

Betts found that a group of psychology students tended to report relatively vivid images (with median scores around 2 or 3 on his 7-point scale), whereas a group of professional psychologists reported less vivid images (with median scores around 4 or 5) (p. 45). Nevertheless, within both of these groups there was considerable individual variation in each of the seven sensory modalities. Finally, there was essentially no relationship between the vividness of reported imagery and the students' academic performance (pp. 31, 48).

Sheehan (1967a) reported that with group testing Betts's QMI took about 55 minutes to administer, which he considered to be prohibitively long for any serious research applications. He therefore developed a shortened form of the QMI that contained just five items from each of the seven sensory modalities and took about 10 minutes to administer, and it is this version of the QMI that has been used in subsequent research. Usually, respondents are assigned mean scores on each of the seven modalities or across the instrument as a whole: low scores are obtained by people who report vivid imagery (sometimes called "good imagers" or "high imagers"), whereas high scores are obtained by people who do not report vivid imagery (sometimes called "poor imagers" or "low imagers"). Sheehan's shortened form of the QMI can be found as Appendix A in the book by A. Richardson (1969, pp. 148–154).

The *reliability* of an instrument such as this (that is, the extent to which it would yield similar results if it were used repeatedly under the same conditions) is usually assessed in two different ways. One way is to measure its *test–retest reliability*: the correlation between the scores obtained when it actually is administered to the same group of people on two different occasions. The second is to measure its *internal consistency*: the degree to which the responses given to the individual items on a single administration correlate with one another. The internal consistency of the shortened form of the QMI tends to be very good, and its test–retest reliability is usually satisfactory (see A. Richardson, 1994, pp. 17–19, 42).

The *validity* of an instrument such as this (that is, the extent to which it is actually measuring what it purports to measure) is also usually assessed in two different ways. One way is to measure its *construct validity*: the degree to which its constituent items are measuring the trait or traits that they are supposed to measure. This often involves the use of factor analysis in order to demonstrate that the instrument has a coherent internal structure or to show that it correlates with other, similar instruments. The second way is to measure its *criterion validity* (sometimes called *predictive validity*): the degree to which scores obtained on the instrument predict people's performance on other tests that are believed to be sensitive to the trait or traits in question.

Fortunately, though not surprisingly, Sheehan (1967a) found that scores obtained on the shortened form of the QMI were highly correlated with the scores obtained by the same individuals on the original QMI. Applications of factor analysis to determine the constituent structure of the shortened form of the QMI tend to produce a primary factor reflecting the vividness of experienced imagery in general, sometimes with secondary factors contrasting particular sensory modalities (see A. Richardson, 1994, pp. 17–18). Nevertheless, attempts to demonstrate the predictive validity of the shortened form of the QMI have been much less successful, as will be discussed in the next section.

In both the original version and the shortened version of the QMI, the items relating to each sensory modality are administered in a single block, and White, Ashton, and Law (1978) suggested that this might induce a response bias to give similar ratings to items within the same modality. They therefore re-worded the 35 items into a common format and reordered them in a random manner so that successive items tapped different sensory modalities. This produced higher ratings (indicating less vivid imagery) overall, which White et al. regarded as evidence for a lenient response bias in the earlier versions of the QMI. However, it also resulted in a "collapsed" factor structure in which two chemical modalities (olfactory and gustatory) loaded on one factor and two mechanical modalities (auditory and cutaneous) loaded on another factor. The randomised version of the shortened form of the QMI can be found in the book by A. Richardson (1994, pp. 128–130).

Using the original QMI, Sheehan (1967a) had found that women tended to report more vivid imagery than men in most of the sensory modalities, but these differences were small and were not statistically significant. A few studies using the shortened form of the QMI have found that women reported more vivid imagery than men; however, these differences, too, are typically small, and in the majority of studies the effects of gender have proved not to be statistically significant (see J.T.E. Richardson, 1991). Ashton and White (1980) reanalysed the data obtained by White et al. (1978) and found no difference at all between the overall vividness ratings of women and men. They concluded that any gender differences obtained on the original shortened version of the QMI were an artefact of blocking the 35 items by sensory modality, in that this led to a bias amongst women to use a more lenient decision criterion in evaluating their experienced mental imagery.

Nevertheless, the failure of White et al. (1978) to obtain a coherent factor structure and the failure of Ashton and White (1980) to obtain a significant overall gender difference on the randomised version of the QMI could equally be regarded as artefacts of randomising the order of the items. It is quite plausible that this would have made it difficult for subjects to use consistent and coherent decision criteria from one item to the next. Let me try to spell this point out more clearly.

Unlike people who participate in interview-based research, people who are asked to fill out questionnaires are unable to calibrate their understanding of the individual items against the meanings that were intended by whoever originally devised the questionnaire or whoever actually administers it to them. Yet, as Strack and Schwarz (1992) demonstrated, the responses that people produce when filling out questionnaires are communicative and collaborative acts which are based upon the same principles as everyday conversation. In the absence of any explicit feedback, the respondents will try to use cues which allow them to infer the questioner's intended meaning for each item, and these cues will typically include the content of the neighbouring items. As a result, randomising the order of the items will remove a major source of information concerning the intended meaning of the individual items and will render the instrument as a whole less intelligible and less reliable.

Marks's Vividness of Visual Imagery Questionnaire

In his initial investigations of the predictive validity of the shortened form of the QMI, Sheehan (1966, 1967b) had some success in correlating the reported vividness of experienced imagery with the accuracy of visual memory. Unfortunately, these results failed to stand up in a more careful replication (Sheehan & Neisser, 1969). Marks (1973) argued that Sheehan's approach was subject to two basic shortcomings. First, he suggested that it was not helpful to assess the vividness of experienced imagery simply by averaging the responses to the QMI across the seven sensory modalities. Instead, it would be more appropriate to assess the modality that was most likely to be used in each particular task. Second, Marks pointed out that Sheehan's experiments had involved remembering abstract geometrical patterns of little inherent interest or meaning to the subjects, and he suggested that vivid imagery would be more likely to be engaged by a more interesting task.

Obviously, in experiments on visual memory, the relevant modality would be vision. Indeed, however the material was to be presented, it could be argued that *visual* imagery would be the most easily aroused and hence would be of most importance in determining people's performance in cognitive tasks. Marks therefore devised the Vividness of Visual Imagery Questionnaire (VVIQ), which contained 16 items (five taken from the original version of the QMI) to be rated in terms of their evoked visual imagery along a 5-point rating scale similar to that used with the QMI. The items themselves concern four familiar objects or scenes, each of which is to be rated on four particular aspects (see Box 2.3). The respondents are assigned mean scores on the basis of their responses across all 16 items. The internal consistency of the VVIQ is good, its test–retest reliability is satisfactory, and the application of factor analysis yields a single underlying dimension. Scores on the VVIQ also tend to be highly correlated with scores on the shortened form of the QMI (see McKelvie, 1995; A. Richardson, 1994, pp. 27, 158).

According to Marks's original specification, the VVIQ is supposed to be completed twice, first with the eyes open and then again with

---

For items 1–4, think of some relative or friend whom you frequently see (but who is not with you at present) and consider carefully the picture that comes before your mind's eye.
Item
  1. The exact contour of face, head, shoulders and body.
  2. Characteristic poses of head, attitudes of body, etc.
  3. The precise carriage, length of step, etc., in walking.
  4. The different colours worn in some familiar clothes.

Visualize a rising sun. Consider carefully the picture that comes before your mind's eye.
Item
  5. The sun is rising above the horizon into a hazy sky.
  6. The sky clears and surrounds the sun with blueness.
  7. Clouds. A storm blows up, with flashes of lightning.
  8. A rainbow appears.

Think of the front of a shop which you often go to. Consider the picture that comes before your mind's eye.
Item
  9. The overall appearance of the shop from the opposite side of the road.
  10. A window display including colours, shapes and details of individual items for sale.
  11. You are near the entrance. The colour, shape and details of the door.
  12. You enter the shop and go to the counter. The counter assistant serves you. Money changes hands.

Finally, think of a country scene which involves trees, mountains and a lake. Consider the picture that comes before your mind's eye.
Item
  13. The contours of the landscape.
  14. The colour and shape of the trees.
  15. The colour and shape of the lake.
  16. A strong wind blows on the trees and on the lake causing waves.

Box 2.3. Vividness of Visual Imagery Questionnaire. From "Visual imagery differences in the recall of pictures", by D.F. Marks, 1973, *British Journal of Psychology*, *64*, 24. Copyright 1973 by the British Psychological Society. Reprinted with permission.

the eyes closed. He provided no rationale for this procedure, but it seems to have been intended to allow for the possibility that visual imagery might be disrupted by concurrent visual perceptions (see Marks, 1983). (This idea will be discussed in more detail in Chapter 3.) The scores that are obtained by individual respondents to the VVIQ do seem to vary slightly, depending upon whether they complete the instrument with their eyes open or closed, but there does not seem to be any systematic difference between the two conditions across different respondents (Isaac & Marks, 1994; McKelvie, 1995). Indeed, some researchers administer the VVIQ once only with no explicit instructions as to whether the respondents' eyes need to be open or closed, while others simply give no indication at all in their published reports as to whether they have followed Marks's original procedure in this regard.

Marks also employed a blocked format in which respondents rated the four aspects of each familiar object or scene before turning to the next. This, he thought, would encourage the natural development of interest and absorption in the rating task. However, in the light of the arguments that had been put forward by White et al. (1978) concerning the shortened form of the QMI, McKelvie (1979) argued that the VVIQ, too, might be vulnerable to a lenient response bias. He devised a randomised version of the VVIQ and confirmed that it too generated higher ratings (indicating less vivid imagery) than the original, blocked version (see McKelvie, 1995). As in the case of the QMI, women tend to report more vivid imagery than men on the original, blocked version of the VVIQ, but there is no gender difference on the randomised version (see Isaac & Marks, 1994; J.T.E. Richardson, 1995b).

One interpretation of these results is that blocking the items in the original version of the VVIQ encourages lenient responding, and that women are more likely to show this lenient response bias than men. Once again, however, it could just as well be argued that the absence of a gender difference on the randomised version of the VVIQ is an artefact of randomising the order of the items, in that this makes it more difficult for the respondents to use consistent and coherent decision criteria from one item to the next. Nothing is known about the impact of randomisation on the VVIQ's factor structure and its predictive capability. However, evidence in favour of the second interpretation comes from the assessment of *split-half reliability*. This is another measure of internal consistency that is based on the correlation between the respondents' mean scores on the odd-numbered items and their mean scores on the even-numbered items.

McKelvie (1986) found that the split-half reliability of the randomised version of the VVIQ was much poorer than that of the original version, and this supports the idea that randomising the item simply makes it harder for people to respond to the VVIQ in a consistent manner.

Marks (1973) carried out three memory experiments in which the materials were coloured photographs of objects or scenes and in which the subjects received a forced-choice recognition test concerned with details of the pictures that had been presented. In each case, people who had been classified as "good visualisers" according to their scores on the original VVIQ produced better performance than people who had been classified as "poor visualisers". In a subsequent experiment, Gur and Hilgard (1975) measured people's reaction times in detecting differences between pairs of pictures that were presented either simultaneously or separated by an interval of 20 seconds. Here, too, the subjects had been classified as "good imagers" or "poor imagers" according to their scores on the original VVIQ. The poor imagers were slower with successive presentation than with simultaneous presentation, but the good imagers were not. Conversely, the good imagers responded more quickly than the poor imagers, but only under conditions of successive presentation. This suggests that imagery is useful for holding pictures in memory over a 20 second interval.

However, these experiments were vulnerable to experimenter effects: that is, the possibility that people who are classified in advance as good or poor imagers may produce the results that the experimenter wants, either because they have become aware of the purpose of the experiment or because they are perhaps quite unconsciously treated differently by the experimenter (Rosenthal, 1966). Such effects can be reduced by using a "double-blind" procedure in which two different experimenters are responsible for identifying the groups of good and poor imagers and for administering the subsequent cognitive task, or by identifying the groups of good and poor imagers *after* the cognitive task has been administered.

Sheehan and Neisser (1969) had used a double-blind procedure in relating subjects' scores on the shortened form of the QMI to their subsequent recall of geometric patterns. They found no correlation between these two variables, but they did find a clear difference between the two experimenters in terms of the imagery ratings that were obtained, and they also found that subjects gave higher ratings after their initial inquiry. Berger and Gaunitz (1977) repeated Gur and Hilgard's (1975) investigation of the relationship between scores on the VVIQ and visual memory, but they identified their groups of good and poor imagers after the memory task had been carried out. They found no sign of any difference in performance between "good imagers" and "poor imagers". Similarly, I found no significant correlation between scores on the shortened form of the QMI and performance in the recall of lists of common nouns when the relevant subject groups were identified after the recall task had been carried out (J.T.E. Richardson, 1978a).

Since the late 1970s, the VVIQ has been used in a very large number of investigations, and McKelvie (1995) provided an integrative review of their findings with regard to its predictive or criterion validity. He found that there was a clear relationship (a mean correlation of +0.377) between rated vividness of mental imagery on the VVIQ and other measures based upon self-reports of mental states. There was a somewhat weaker but still appreciable relationship (a mean correlation of +0.273) between rated vividness of mental imagery on the VVIQ and objective performance in cognitive or perceptual tasks. Finally, there was only a relatively weak relationship (a mean correlation of +0.137) between rated vividness of mental imagery on the VVIQ and objective performance in tests of learning and memory. Indeed, in certain tasks that demand relatively fine judgements about the physical properties of familiar people or objects, there tends to be a negative relationship between rated vividness of mental imagery on the VVIQ and performance; this effect apparently arises because good imagers are unable to differentiate between bona fide memories and plausible fictions (B.H. Cohen & Saslona, 1990; Reisberg, Culver, Heuer, & Fischman, 1986; Reisberg & Leak, 1987).

Isaac, Marks, and Russell (1986) developed an instrument analogous to the VVIQ to measure differences in motor imagery, the Vividness of Movement Imagery Questionnaire (VMIQ). This describes 24 activities that are to be rated twice: first with regard to the vividness of an image of another person carrying out the action, and then again with regard to the vividness of an image of performing it oneself. The test–retest reliability of this instrument was found to be satisfactory, and the total score was found to be highly correlated with that on the VVIQ. Isaac and Marks (1994) found differences on both the VVIQ and the VMIQ in children with poor movement control, students who were taking courses in physical education, élite athletes, pilots, and air traffic controllers when compared with relevant control subjects. They inferred that differences in experienced imagery were systematically linked to skilled perceptual-motor performance. However, their data were correlational in nature, and the findings could therefore mean that skilled performance is responsible for vivid imagery, rather than vice versa.

Gordon's Test of Visual Imagery Control

Despite the fact that Galton (1880) characterised vivid mental imagery as "antagonistic to the acquirement of habits of highly generalised and abstract thought" (p. 304), he conceded that it could be helpful in carrying out cognitive tasks to the extent that it could be controlled and manipulated; in other words, when it was "duly subordinated to the higher intellectual operations". Elsewhere, he argued that visual imagery would be particularly beneficial for planning and problem solving "in every handicraft and profession where design is required" and "in all technical and artistic occupations", including scientific experimentation (Galton, 1883, pp. 113–114).

Gordon (1949) devised a questionnaire containing 11 questions to be answered in a yes/no manner with the aim of classifying the respondents in terms of whether their imagery tended to be "controlled" or "autonomous". (Her own interest was in the extent to which this affected how strongly the respondents held stereotypes of particular cultural groups.) Start and A. Richardson (1964) amended this questionnaire by changing one of the original items into two separate items, by including an "unsure" response category, and finally by standardising the instructions (see A. Richardson, 1969, pp. 58, 155–156). This revised instrument is nowadays usually known as the (Gordon) Test of Visual Imagery Control (TVIC), although A. Richardson (1994, pp. 29–32, 152–153) described it as the Controllability of Visual Imagery Questionnaire. The 12 questions are shown in Box 2.4. If "Yes" responses are scored as 2, "Unsure" responses as 1, and "No" responses as 0, the TVIC produces a distribution of total scores ranging from 0 to 24.

The internal consistency of this instrument is good, and its test–retest reliability is satisfactory. However, given that the 12 questions are restricted to the visual modality, it is perhaps surprising that the TVIC appears to have a complex internal structure. Applications of factor analysis typically give rise to four separate, albeit correlated factors:

1. Can you see a car standing in the road in front of a house?
2. Can you see it in colour?
3. Can you now see it in a different colour?
4. Can you now see the same car lying upside down?
5. Can you now see the same car back on its four wheels again?
6. Can you see the car running along the road?
7. Can you see it climb up a very steep hill?
8. Can you see it climb over the top?
9. Can you see it get out of control and crash through a house?
10. Can you now see the same car running along the road with a handsome couple inside?
11. Can you see the car cross a bridge and fall over the side into the stream below?
12. Can you see the car all old and dismantled in a car cemetery?

Box 2.4. The Gordon Test of Visual Imagery Control. From *Mental Imagery* (p. 156), by A. Richardson, 1969, London: Routledge & Kegan Paul. Adapted with permission from "An investigation into some of the factors that favour the formation of stereotyped images," by R. Gordon, 1949, *British Journal of Psychology, 39*, 158. Copyright 1949 by the British Psychological Society and 1969 by Routledge & Kegan Paul. Reprinted with permission.

- movement (items 6, 7, and 8);
- misfortune (items 4, 9, 11, and 12);
- colour (items 2, 3, and 10);
- stationary (items 1, 5, and possibly 4).

Scores on the TVIC tend to be correlated with scores on both the VVIQ and the shortened form of the QMI. They also show a positive relationship to measures of creative thinking, but in the relatively few studies that have been carried out they have not been consistently related to performance on tests of memory and cognitive function (see McKelvie, 1995; A. Richardson, 1994, pp. 29–32, 60, 80, 82, 90–94, 159, 160). Finally, some researchers have found a (usually non-significant) tendency for women to produce higher scores on the TVIC than men, but others have found no gender difference at all (see J.T.E. Richardson, 1991).

The role of imagery in cognition

At the same time as Galton was collecting questionnaire responses on the distribution of mental imagery, Wundt was establishing the first research institute for the study of experimental psychology in Leipzig. His work was based upon relatively simple psychophysical experiments, but he also introduced the technique of asking subjects to report on their experience whilst carrying out the tasks in question. As Fancher (1994, pp. 29–30) pointed out, Wundt himself had grave reservations about the value of this "introspective" method and regarded it mainly as a way of generating hypotheses that could subsequently be tested by non-introspective methods. Perhaps most important, Wundt believed that complex mental processes such as thinking and remembering could never be adequately studied *either* by introspection *or* by experimentation.

Nevertheless, some of Wundt's students developed this approach far beyond the analysis of simple mental episodes. In particular, Titchener maintained that all forms of mental experience, however complex, could be analysed in terms of certain basic elements, and that these would be revealed by asking subjects to report on their mental processes whilst carrying out cognitive tasks. As Holt (1964) commented, mental images were identified as the most obvious elements into which thought processes might be introspectively analysed. However, similar research carried out by Külpe failed to substantiate these conclusions. When performing even relatively simple cognitive acts such as giving word associations or judging the comparative weight of two objects, Külpe's subjects could often report either no conscious experience at all or else simply one of indescribable or "imageless" thought.

The "imageless thought controversy" helped to foster a move away from the use of introspection and towards the systematic study and measurement of behaviour. In the United States, this reaction took an extreme form in the behaviourist movement. The behaviour-ists argued that mental phenomena by their very nature could not be the object of scientific investigation, and so the study of behaviour should be the sole aim of psychology (see, for example, Watson, 1914). This view came to dominate research in human experimental psychology (in English-speaking countries, at least) from the 1920s to the 1950s. Consequently, although psychologists involved in phe-nomenological or clinical research continued to investigate mental imagery, there was very little development during this period in understanding its role in human cognition.

With the rise of modern cognitive psychology during the 1960s, however, it became possible once again to reinstate mental imagery as a legitimate object of scientific investigation. The moral of the imageless thought controversy is that it cannot be assumed that imagery plays a fundamental causal role in all forms of human cognition. Instead, most researchers are content to assume that cognition involves both imaginal and non-imaginal representations. The interesting project is therefore to determine the circumstances in which these different representations are used and the nature of the interface between them. Partly because of the legacy of behaviourism, most researchers have chosen to pursue this by means of non-introspective methods, and their work will be described in the following chapter. Nevertheless, some studies have focused upon the phenomenal properties of mental imagery in representing information.

In modern times, this idea was first raised by Shepard (1966), who commented that, in order to count the number of windows in his house, he had to picture the house from different sides or from within different rooms and then count the windows portrayed in these various mental images. Most people seem to concur with Shepard's account of how he would answer this question. Moreover, as one would expect, there is a direct, linear relationship between the time taken to answer this question and the number of windows that are actually counted (Meudell, 1971). Berlyne (1965, p. 142) similarly argued that imagery would have to be used in recalling a linear series of geographical locations (such as the US states one would pass over when flying from San Francisco to New York). Once again, in this situation there is a direct, linear relationship between the number of locations named and the time taken to name them, much as if people are reading the locations from an actual map (Indow & Togano, 1970).

Finke (1989) characterised this property of mental imagery as the "implicit encoding principle":

> Mental imagery is instrumental in retrieving information about the physical properties of objects, or about physical relationships among objects, that was not explicitly encoded at any previous time. (p. 7)

However, underpinning this is a separate property that Finke characterised as the "principle of structural equivalence":

> The structure of mental images corresponds to that of actual perceived objects, in the sense that the structure is coherent, well organized, and can be reorganized and reinterpreted. (p. 120)

Finke reviewed experimental research which demonstrated that people can come to recognise properties of objects imaged in either a viewer-centred manner (how the object appears from a particular vantage point) or in an object-centred manner (in terms of the object's inherent, three-dimensional structure).

Nevertheless, there are some limitations on this process of reinterpretation, particularly when people try to detect structurally "hidden" parts within complex line drawings or to detect perceptual

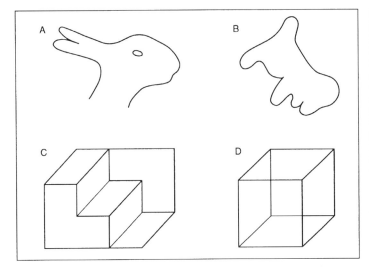

FIG. 2.1. Examples of perceptually reversible figures used in Chambers and Reisberg's (1985) experiments on reinterpreting mental images. A is the "duck/rabbit", B is the "dog/chef", C is the Schroder staircase, and D is the Necker cube. From "Can mental images be ambiguous?" by D. Chambers and D. Reisberg, 1985, *Journal of Experimental Psychology: Human Perception and Performance, 11,* 320. Copyright © 1985 by the American Psychological Association.

reversals of ambiguous figures. Figure 2.1 shows four classical ambiguous figures: the "duck/rabbit" figure; the "chef/dog" figure; the Schroder staircase; and the Necker cube. If you look at each of these figures for a while, you should see the first figure alternately as a duck and as a rabbit and the second figure alternately as a chef (facing down to the left) and as a dog (facing down to the right), while the third and fourth figures will reverse in their apparent depth.

In contrast, Chambers and Reisberg (1985) found that, when people were asked to make up a mental image of one of these figures and to try to construe it differently, they were unable to do so: in other words, they could "see" the figure from only one of the two possible views. Yet, when they were asked to draw the figure from memory, all the participants could report both views once they studied their drawings. As Chambers and Reisberg noted, they were able to create an ambiguous picture from an unambiguous image. Subsequent investigations showed that reinterpreting mental images is not wholly impossible, but that it demands specific training, instructions, and prompting (Brandimonte & Gerbino, 1993; Hyman, 1993; Kaufmann & Helstrup, 1993; Peterson, Kihlstrom, Rose, & Glisky, 1992). This is quite a complex issue that has important implications for the role of imagery in creative thinking, and it was discussed in detail by Cornoldi, Logie, Brandimonte, Kaufmann, and Reisberg (1996).

As Galton (1883) had originally suggested, there seem to be a variety of situations in which it is helpful or even essential to be able to "read off" visual or spatial information from a mental image. Nevertheless, the results of these studies have the more specific implication that an image is a relatively faithful model of the perceptual information on which it is based. To evaluate this idea, Kosslyn (1973) asked people to memorise drawings of objects (for instance, a drawing of a boat with a motor at the stern, a porthole in the middle and an anchor at the bow). They were then instructed to visualise a drawing, to focus their attention on one end of the object (such as the end with the motor) and to say whether the drawing had contained a specific part (such as an anchor). The time taken to scan to the relevant location increased with the actual distance to be scanned.

This sort of finding was confirmed in several subsequent investigations. For instance, Pinker and Kosslyn (1978) found that the time taken mentally to scan between two objects in a memorised scene increased in a direct linear fashion with the actual distance in three dimensions between the objects. This indicates that mental images can capture the metric structure of Euclidean space. Moreover, Denis and Cocude (1989) obtained a similar relationship between distance and scanning time even if mental images had to be generated from verbal descriptions. In one condition, they asked subjects to memorise the map of a fictitious circular island with six landmarks on its coast; in another condition, a different group of subjects listened to a text that described the positions of the landmarks in relation to the island's centre:

> The island is circular in shape. Six features are situated at its periphery. At 11 o'clock, there is a harbour. At 1, there is a lighthouse. At 2, there is a creek. Equidistant from 2 and 3, there is a hut. At 4, there is a beach. At 7, there is a cave. (p. 296)

Both groups of subjects were asked to visualise the map and to scan between pairs of landmarks in their mental image. In both cases, scanning time varied directly with the distance scanned. However, when the image had to be constructed from a text, the degree of association between scanning time and distance varied with the number of times that the subjects had been allowed to listen to the text to learn the configuration of landmarks. In a subsequent experiment, Denis and Cocude (1992) showed that it also varied with the structural coherence of the text. In both these studies, the strength of the association between distance and scanning time appeared to depend upon the uncertainty that was associated with the location of the landmarks, and learning the verbal description consisted in reducing this uncertainty.

It is, in principle, possible that findings such as these result from experimenter effects of the sort that I mentioned earlier. A number of researchers have shown that the actual response times in mental-scanning experiments do vary with the experimenters' expectations (see, for example, Intons-Peterson, 1983). Nevertheless, the basic association between farther distances and longer scanning times does not appear to vary in this way. Consequently, it seems to reflect inherent properties of the representation that is being used and the processes that operate upon it (Kosslyn, 1994, pp. 10–11).

Finke (1989) characterised this property of mental imagery as the "principle of spatial equivalence":

> The spatial arrangement of the elements of a mental image corresponds to the way objects or their parts are arranged on actual physical surfaces or in an actual physical space. (p. 61)

The loss of mental imagery

Given that the occurrence of mental imagery has to be inferred from people's verbal accounts, from a neuropsychological point of view an interesting phenomenon would be reports of the loss of mental imagery in patients who had suffered brain damage or disease. Ehrlichman and Barrett (1983) noted that the clinical literature contained only a small number of case reports in which the loss of imagery was the patient's salient complaint. They summarised the findings and implications of these reports in the following way:

> First, loss of imagery is probably rare. Second, reports of loss of imagery are not contingent on damage to the right hemisphere. If anything, it is damage to the posterior areas of the left hemisphere that is more often associated with reported loss of imagery. (p. 61)

Basso, Bisiach, and Luzzatti (1980) noted that in many cases the subjective complaint of loss of imagery was restricted to the visual modality, although this could encompass intentional imagining, dreaming, and hypnagogic experiences (that is, images experienced whilst falling asleep).

In Chapter 1, I referred to Kosslyn's (1980) componential analysis of visual imagery. This postulates a long-term visual memory containing stored information about the appearance of physical objects and a short-term "visual buffer", which is the medium in which images actually occur. A complex generation process creates an image in the visual buffer from information stored within long-term visual memory. (I shall describe this model in more detail in Chapter 3.) Farah (1984) reviewed the clinical literature on loss of imagery in terms of Kosslyn's model, and she identified 27 patients in whom there was sound documentation of an impaired imagery system.

The patterns of deficits and residual abilities shown by these patients suggested that in eight instances there was a selective impairment of the image generation process. In six of these patients, there was evidence that their brain damage was predominantly or exclusively restricted to the posterior portion of the cerebral hemisphere which was specialised for language function (usually the left hemisphere). Farah inferred that "the critical area for image generation may be close to the posterior language centers of the left hemisphere" (p. 268). An additional four cases with similar deficits were described by Farah, Levine, and Calvanio (1988), but Sergent (1990) expressed scepticism about the evidence of localisation in many of the cases described by Farah and her colleagues.

In 13 other patients, the pattern of deficits and residual abilities suggested damage to the representations which were stored in long-term visual memory, and possibly to the image generation process as well. This pattern was associated with damage to one or both of the occipital lobes. In one further patient, there was insufficient documentation to determine to which of these categories he should be assigned. Each of the five remaining patients had suffered from extensive damage to both cerebral hemispheres. They were profoundly impaired in describing or copying physical objects, whether the objects in question were physically present or were to be visualised from memory. Farah ascribed this kind of impairment to a defective image inspection process.

One group of patients who should be especially interesting in this context are "split-brain" patients (see Chapter 1). As Ehrlichman and Barrett (1983) noted, it should be a relatively straightforward matter to find out whether patients with split brains are able to generate, utilise, and report mental imagery solely within the left hemisphere. In the following chapters, I shall describe research evidence on the objective performance of split-brain patients, but unfortunately there has been very little systematic investigation of their phenomenal experience. What one can say is that complaints of a loss of mental imagery do not seem to figure in careful accounts of the symptomatology and cognitive functioning of these patients (see, for instance, Gazzaniga & LeDoux, 1978). Based on the limited evidence that was available, Ehrlichman and Barrett themselves concluded that the surgically isolated left cerebral hemisphere "is capable of generating and experiencing visual imagery in dreams" (p. 65).

Brain activity during imagery

Additional evidence on the neural mechanisms involved in image generation comes from research using physiological recording. Davidson and Schwartz (1977) measured the EEG alpha rhythm over the occipital and parietal regions of the brain. When their subjects were instructed to make up visual images (by imagining a flashing light), there was attenuation of the alpha rhythm (implying increased brain activity) over the occipital region. However, when the subjects were instructed to make up tactile images (by imagining their forearm being tapped), there was attenuation of the alpha rhythm across the parietal region.

A subsequent experiment by Farah, Péronnet, Weisberg, and Perrin (described in Farah, 1988) measured event-related potentials (ERPs). This compared the ERPs produced in response to visually presented words in two different conditions: in one condition, subjects were asked to make up images of the things described by the words; in the second, control condition, they were simply asked to read the words. Farah et al. found that in the former condition (i.e. under imagery instructions) there was "a highly localized increase in positivity of the ERP . . . at the occipital electrodes, implicating occipital activity during the process of imaging" (p. 311).

Marks, Tatsuno, Uemura, Ashida, and Imamura (described in Marks, 1990) recorded the EEG alpha rhythm at 12 different locations across the scalp while their subjects generated mental images in response to the 16 items in the VVIQ. The subjects were volunteers who had been selected from a sample of 100 students on the basis of their extreme scores on an earlier administration of the VVIQ, although in the experiment itself no overt responses were required. Four subjects who had been classified as "vivid imagers" exhibited widespread symmetrical activation in the frontal, temporal, and parietal cortex. As Marks (1990) pointed out, these results in themselves "provide clear disconfirmation of the hypothesis which makes imagery a specialization of the right hemisphere" (p. 28). Four subjects who had been classified as "non-vivid imagers" showed a focus in the right prefrontal area, but this was somewhat difficult to interpret. A comparison between the two patterns of activity produced statistically significant differences only in the left occipito-parietal cortex: in other words, vivid imagers produced more activation than non-vivid imagers in the posterior region of the left hemisphere.

Goldenberg, Podreka, and Steiner (1990) described an informal case study in which the pattern of regional cerebral blood flow was measured while the subject (the first author) was engaged in daydreaming. Here, too, the area of increased activity was the occipital cortex, the maximum regional flow being in the left inferior occipital region. Nevertheless, a subsequent experiment produced more complicated results. The subjects were presented with a tape-recorded list of letters of the alphabet, and they were required to report (by flashing a light) the number of corners contained in an outline version of each letter when printed in upper-case type. Afterwards, they received the VVIQ and were also specifically asked to rate the vividness of the letters they had imagined during the course of the experiment. Regional blood flow in 18 subjects carrying out this task was compared with that in a control condition which involved counting the numbers of letters separating two presented letters in the alphabet.

While the "corners" task produced a slight increase in brain activity in both inferior temporal regions and in the left inferior occipital region, this effect was statistically far from reliable. The number of significant correlations between overall ratings of visual imagery and the blood flow in different regions did not exceed that which would have been expected by chance. However, there were clear and significant associations between regional cerebral blood flow during the "corners" task and the vividness of visual imagery experienced during the task. Specifically, the rated vividness of experienced imagery was positively related to brain activity in the inferior temporal regions, and there was a similar, though somewhat weaker, relationship with brain activity in the inferior occipital regions.

Marks and Isaac (1995) selected 16 subjects as either "vivid" or "non-vivid" imagers on the basis of their scores on the VVIQ and the VMIQ (the analogous questionnaire on movement imagery). Five different EEG frequency bands were measured at 16 different locations across the scalp while the subjects generated mental images in response to the first four items in the VVIQ. These measures were then aggregated to estimate EEG activity within four quadrants of the brain (left and right frontal regions and left and right posterior regions). There was suppression of the alpha rhythm mainly within the left posterior quadrant, but this occurred only in the vivid imagers and was not apparent in the non-vivid imagers. The results were taken to support the idea of a module responsible for image generation located in the left cerebral hemisphere.

Several of the studies that have been described thus far suggested that the occipital lobe was activated during the phenomenal experience of visual imagery. The occipital lobe contains the region of the brain that is responsible for the initial analysis of visually perceived information, known as the primary visual cortex. This therefore raises the question whether the generation of images might even involve mechanisms within the primary visual cortex (Kosslyn et al., 1993). Mellet, Tzourio, Denis, and Mazoyer (1995) employed positron emission tomography to measure changes in regional cerebral blood flow whilst their subjects mentally explored a visual image of a previously learned map. Mellet et al. found evidence for the activation of several regions, including the superior occipital cortex, the supplementary motor area, and the cerebellum (the illustration on the front cover of this volume is an example), but no evidence for involvement of the primary visual cortex.

D'Esposito et al. (1997) addressed this question using functional MRI. In one condition the subjects heard concrete nouns (such as *apple*, *house*, and *horse*) and were instructed to make up images of the named objects. In another condition the subjects heard abstract nouns (such as *treaty*, *guilt*, and *tenure*) and were instructed to listen passively while they were presented. By comparing the patterns of activation in the two conditions, D'Esposito et al. sought to identify the brain regions involved in the generation of mental images. Across seven subjects, the most consistently activated region was the left inferior temporal lobe, although in some subjects the area of activation extended into the left lateral occipital lobe. There are two problems with this study: (a) the presentation rate of one item per second may have been too fast to allow the subjects to generate adequate images; and (b) the use of imagery was confounded with the concreteness of the words presented, which may be linked to variables unrelated to image processing (see Chapter 4). Nevertheless, the findings clearly implicate the visual association cortex rather than the primary visual cortex in the process of image generation.

One final consideration is that it is apparently possible to induce imaginal experiences by the direct application of weak electrical stimulation to the brain. This technique was used by Penfield and Perot (1963) in order to determine the area of focal damage in cases of temporal-lobe epilepsy. When stimulation was applied under local anaesthesia to the surface of the temporal lobes, the patients often reported the occurrence of auditory and visual hallucinations, which at least in some cases appeared to take the form of "flash-backs" of previous autobiographical events. Similar reports of "memory-like hallucinations" were obtained by Halgren, Walter, Cherlow and Crandall (1978) and by Gloor, Olivier, Quesney, Andermann, and Horowitz (1982) using electrodes implanted in the limbic system, which is a complex network of pathways concerned with the expression of emotion and motivation.

These reports were associated especially with stimulation of the amygdala and the hippocampus, which are structures in the temporal lobes thought to be involved in human learning and memory. Penfield and Perot suggested that these hallucinatory episodes were based upon the mental record of actual past experiences (see also Penfield, 1968). However, Loftus and Loftus (1980) argued that they consisted merely of thoughts and ideas which happened to occur prior to and during stimulation. Penfield and Perot also reported that these experiences were more likely to be elicited by stimulation of the right temporal lobe than by stimulation of the left temporal lobe, but Gloor et al. (1982) could find no sign of such a difference between the responsiveness of the two hemispheres.

Summary: Imagery as a phenomenal experience

1. As a phenomenal experience, imagery has to be studied through verbal accounts. A number of questionnaires have been devised for evaluating experienced imagery, of which the most widely used is probably the VVIQ.
2. Scores on these instruments show satisfactory levels of reliability and internal consistency, and scores on different instruments are highly correlated.

3. These scores show only a modest relationship with objective performance on cognitive or perceptual tasks and only a weak relationship with performance in tests of learning and memory. However, mental images have functional properties that should enable them to be useful in a wide range of cognitive tasks.
4. Reports of the loss of imagery as a phenomenal experience following brain damage do not appear to be related to damage to the right cerebral hemisphere or to surgical separation of the two hemispheres.
5. Such reports do seem to be linked to damage to the posterior portion of the left cerebral hemisphere. This notion has received some support from research using physiological recording techniques, although research using brain imaging technology suggests that structures in both hemispheres may be involved. The relevant structures include those within the superior and lateral occipital lobes but apparently not the primary visual cortex.

Imagery as an internal representation 3

In Chapter 2, I raised the idea that mental images served as relatively faithful models of a perceptual object, event, or scene from which it might be possible to "read off" relevant visual or spatial information. The key notion here is that mental images possess "emergent" properties that could not be readily calculated, computed, or deduced simply from abstract descriptions of the object, event, or scene in question (see Rollins, 1989, Chapter 5). The example that I gave was that of counting the number of windows in one's house by "reading off" the information from mental images depicting different views of the outside of the house or different rooms within the house.

It follows that mental imagery is not simply a phenomenal experience, but a medium or a form of internal representation in which information about the appearance of physical objects, events, and scenes can be depicted and manipulated. As a consequence, mental imagery is able to make a distinctive contribution to performance in objectively scorable tasks, and these are normally characterised as tests of "spatial ability". Indeed, for some researchers the importance of imagery as a theoretical construct is determined solely by its predictive validity or criterion validity (in other words, its capacity to predict objective performance), and whether or not it is open to conscious introspection is wholly irrelevant.

Tests of spatial ability

"Spatial ability" is a rather vague, catch-all description that is used to describe a very diverse collection of tasks which plausibly can only be carried out by manipulating some visual or spatial representation rather than more abstract linguistic information. In spite of this vagueness, psychologists have usually assumed that mental imagery is an important component of such tasks. For instance, while Harris (1978) noted that "spatial ability" had been variously defined by researchers, he suggested that "each characterization implies mental imagery, but of a distinctly kinetic rather than static kind" (p. 287).

Some researchers have tried to refine this concept by identifying different kinds of spatial ability. For instance, Linn and Petersen (1985) proposed the following classification:

- In *spatial perception* tests, subjects are required to determine spatial relationships with respect to the orientation of their own bodies in the face of distracting information. Examples of this include the Rod and Frame Test and the Water Level Test.
- In *mental rotation* tests, subjects are required mentally to rotate two- or three-dimensional figures quickly and accurately. Examples of this include the Cards Rotation Test and the Spatial Relations subtest of the Primary Mental Abilities Test. Other writers have called these tests of "spatial orientation".
- In *spatial visualisation* tests, subjects are required to solve problems by manipulating complex spatial information through several discrete stages. Examples include the Embedded Figures Test and the Minnesota Paper Form Board.

Linn and Petersen found this classification helpful in making sense of the literature on gender differences in spatial ability. They found that, in general, men tended to outperform women on spatial tests; the effects tended to be large and consistent on tests of mental rotation, large but somewhat less consistent on tests of spatial perception, and highly variable and often not statistically significant on tests of spatial visualisation. Voyer, Voyer, and Bryden (1995) obtained very similar results, but they found that gender differences varied even between different tests of the same type. They concluded that Linn and Petersen's classification of spatial tests was still somewhat arbitrary and in need of further refinement.

Nevertheless, scores obtained on different tests of spatial ability tend to correlate moderately well with one another, and they load on the same factor or factors when factor analysis is applied to scores obtained on a battery of such tests. On the other hand, objective performance on tests of spatial ability does not show any consistent relationship with subjective ratings of the vividness of experienced imagery obtained by means of questionnaires of the sort reviewed in Chapter 2, and the two sorts of instrument typically load on different factors in the results of factor analyses (see McKelvie, 1995; J.T.E. Richardson, 1980b, pp. 130–131). Moreover, whereas men tend to outperform women on tests of spatial ability, it will be recalled from Chapter 2 that women tend to report more vivid imagery than men.

These results suggest that the functional value or effectiveness of mental imagery in tests of spatial ability is probably unrelated to the vividness of experienced imagery.

If, however, as Harris (1978) argued, tests of spatial ability involve the use of mental imagery, then the important consideration should be not the quality of experienced imagery in general, but the quality of the imagery that is experienced whilst carrying out a particular spatial task. This was first considered by Betts (1909), who asked a class of 28 psychology students to solve the problems shown in Box 3.1. After each problem, he asked them to rate the clearness and vividness of any images which had come to mind, using the 7-point scale that he had devised for his Questionnaire upon Mental Imagery (QMI), which was described in Chapter 2. The majority of the subjects managed to solve these problems, and nearly all reported using imagery to do so. This contrasted with the much less frequent reports of imagery obtained following other tasks, and so Betts concluded that imagery was only of use in situations ''where we would be glad to use percepts but find them lacking'' (p. 98).

Similarly, Barratt (1953) administered a battery of 12 psychometric tests to a total of 180 schoolboys of between 14 and 19 years of age. After each test, the subjects were asked to look back through the test items and to rate the vividness, importance, and manipulability of the visual images which they had experienced in tackling the various problems (see Box 3.2). Although, in retrospect, it might have been interesting to compare the three scales, Barratt simply calculated the total rating for each subject on each test across all three scales, combined these ratings across different groups of tests, and compared the subjects whose combined imagery ratings on each group of tests fell in the highest 25% (whom he called ''high imagers'') with those whose combined imagery ratings fell in the lowest 25% (whom he called ''low imagers'').

Box 3.1.
Two problems set by Betts (1909). From *The Distribution and Functions of Mental Imagery* (pp. 70–71), by G.H. Betts, 1909, New York: Columbia University, Teachers College. Copyright © 1909 by Teachers College Press. Reprinted with permission.

---

1. A squirrel is clinging to one side of a tree, and a man is standing opposite on the other side of the tree. The man walks around the tree, but the squirrel also moves around the tree, so as to keep just out of the man's sight. They continue this movement until each has gone entirely around the tree. Has the man gone around the squirrel,
   a. in the sense of having been in front, behind, and on both sides of him?
   b. in the sense of having been east, west, north and south of him?

2. A three-inch cube, painted red, is sawn into inch cubes.
   a. How many of the inch cubes have paint on three faces?
   b. How many on two faces?
   c. How many on one face?
   d. How many have no paint on them?

Box 3.2.
The rating scale of
visual imagery used
by Barratt (1953).
From: pp. 158–159
of "Imagery and
thinking", by P.E.
Barratt, 1953,
*Australian Journal
of Psychology*, 5,
pp. 154–164.
Copyright © 1953
The Australian
Psychological
Society Ltd.

1. Strength and clearness of images visualised

In solving the problems of this test did you visualise the figures and/or component parts, holding them as a sort of "picture in the head" during the solution process? Or, at the moment of solution did you "see" the result, e.g. the completed figure, the figure in a new position, the assembled parts etc. as a whole. In any of these cases were your visualisations

(a) almost photographic in strength and clearness of detail.
(b) strong and clear with shape and form defined.
(c) clearly present, rich in essential detail.
(d) moderately clear with some detail.
(e) present as a general impression only.
(f) vague and ill-defined.
(g) absent altogether.

2. Importance and use of visualisation in solution

In solving the problems of this test did you MAKE USE of whatever visualising was present in getting the relations between the shapes, forms, spaces. Were visual images an essential part of the process? Did they help you? Did you feel, "This would be easy if I could get a clear picture of it and hold it in my head"? Did you deliberately try to get images as your method of approach? How important were they?

(a) The most important factor in solution.
(b) A major factor in solution.
(c) Definitely used, along with other important factors.
(d) Of some use in solution.
(e) Of minor importance in an incidental way.
(f) Of no use at all, purely incidental if present.
(g) A hindrance to solution—just "got in the way."

3. Facility of manipulation of visualisations

In the solution of the problems of this test, did you find yourself manipulating the figures and/or parts in visual imagery, juggling them into various positions, turning them around and over, forging new combinations, imaging how they would look in such and such a position, in a kind of mental trial and error? With what facility was this manipulation effected? Try to consider this apart from the inherent difficulty of the item.

(a) Manipulation of images almost as easy as that of real objects.
(b) Manipulation easy and effortless.
(c) Manipulation not difficult but required some effort.
(d) Manipulation only effected with some difficulty.
(e) Manipulation difficult to the point of creating tension.
(f) Manipulation scarcely possible. Feelings of frustration?
(g) Manipulation impossible.

When the subjects were compared in terms of their combined imagery ratings on all 12 tests, the high imagers obtained a higher mean score than the low imagers on every test. However, in itself, this result was difficult to interpret because the difference was statistically significant for only seven of the 12 tests. In a pilot study, Barratt had carried out a factor analysis which indicated that the 12 tests could be divided into at least two different groups: one was concerned with "spatial manipulation" and combined tests of mental rotation with tests of spatial visualisation; a second was concerned with (non-verbal) reasoning. Barratt found that in general his subjects gave much higher imagery ratings to the tests in the first group than to the tests in the second group. Moreover, when they were compared in terms of their combined imagery ratings solely within each group of tests, the high imagers produced significantly higher scores than the low imagers on every test of spatial manipulation, but there was no sign of any difference on any of the tests of reasoning.

A. Richardson (1977a) also administered a battery of tests and self-report instruments to groups of university students. One of these was Betts's (1909) "cutting a cube" task (see Box 3.1), which in the intervening period had become widely used as a test of spatial visualisation (see, for instance, Guilford, Fruchter, & Zimmerman, 1952). Richardson gave the following instructions:

> Imagine a cube 3in × 3in × 3in and painted red all over. Now imagine that it has been cut into 27 smaller cubes each 1in × 1in × 1in by making two equidistant vertical cuts and two equidistant horizontal cuts. Your task is to answer the following questions: "How many cubes have three faces painted red? How many cubes have two faces painted red? How many cubes have one face painted red? How many cubes have no faces painted red?" (p. 33)

Following this task, the subjects were asked to assess the clarity of any associated images and the ease with which the imagery aroused by the task could be manipulated, using rating scales based upon those devised by Barratt (1953).

Data were obtained from a total of 81 students. Their scores on the "cutting a cube" task were highly correlated with the vividness of their imagery while carrying out the task but were not significantly correlated with the controllability of their imagery while carrying out the task, with the vividness of their imagery in general according to the shortened form of the QMI, or with the controllability of their imagery according to the Test of Visual Imagery Control (TVIC). One problem with this study, however, is that the instructions quoted above are inaccurate: as Lorenz and Neisser (1985) pointed out, the four cuts described would result in nine cuboids, each measuring 1in × 1in × 3in, rather than 27 cubes. Did you spot this?

Hiscock (1978) devised a Visual Manipulation Scale which contained "cutting a cube" and other tasks requiring the mental manipulation of imaginary objects. Consistent with Richardson's results, Hiscock found that the performance of 79 subjects on this scale was largely unrelated to their scores on the TVIC or to their scores on the visual and auditory scales of the QMI. Nevertheless, their performance on this scale was significantly correlated with their scores on the Minnesota Paper Form Board, the spatial visualisation test that was mentioned earlier. When a factor analysis was carried out on these and other measures, the scores on the Visual Manipulation Scale and the Minnesota Paper Form Board defined a single factor that was distinct from measures based upon self-reports such as the QMI and the TVIC.

Lorenz and Neisser (1985) carried out a similar study that involved 58 students. Their battery of instruments included two tests of spatial ability: one was the Space Relations Form of the Differential Aptitude Test; the other was the "cutting a cube" task. In each case, the subjects were asked to rate the vividness, importance, and manipulability of the visual images they had experienced while carrying out the relevant test using Barratt's questionnaire. Lorenz and Neisser also administered three of the instruments that were discussed in Chapter 2: the shortened form of the QMI, the Vividness of Visual Imagery Questionnaire (VVIQ), and the TVIC, plus a parallel form of the TVIC in which the subjects were asked to form an image of a snowmobile rather than a car. The total ratings on the two applications of Barratt's questionnaire were found to be highly correlated, and so they were combined into a single score. Performance on both of the spatial tests was found to be significantly correlated with the combined imagery ratings on Barratt's questionnaire, but it was essentially unrelated to the subjects' scores on the QMI, the VVIQ, and the TVIC.

These results are of course correlational in nature, and it cannot therefore be inferred that differences in experienced imagery gave rise to differences in performance. For instance, it is possible that the subjects simply gave higher or lower ratings on the basis of how successful they had been on each test (in which case differences in performance would have given rise to differences in their reports of experienced imagery). However, as Barratt (1953) himself pointed out, in this case it is extremely odd that a similar correlation was not obtained in the case of his tests of reasoning. It is much simpler to explain these findings by supposing that experienced imagery is employed in carrying out tests of spatial manipulation but is of very little importance in carrying out tests of reasoning.

One can also enquire whether spatial manipulation ability predicts the ease with which people can make use of imagery. In Chapter 2, I referred to experiments involving the scanning of mental images that had been derived from perceived displays or generated from verbal descriptions. The results showed that the time taken mentally to scan between two objects in a memorised display increased in a direct linear fashion with the actual physical distance between the objects. This implied that mental imagery was a fairly literal representation which captured the metric structure of three-dimensional Euclidean space.

Denis and Cocude (1997) asked 32 subjects to scan images of a fictitious island generated on the basis of a short text that described the relative locations of a number of landmarks. Amongst these subjects, they classified those who had obtained the highest and lowest scores on the Minnesota Paper Form Board as a group of 12 "high visuo-spatial imagers" and a group of 12 "low visuo-spatial imagers", respectively. The former subjects produced faster overall scanning times than the latter, but the groups also differed in the strength of the association between distance and scanning time. The high imagers produced a clear, highly significant relationship ($r = 0.84$), but the low imagers produced only a weak and nonsignificant relationship ($r = 0.32$). This indicated that people with relatively high spatial ability are better able to generate and explore mental representations that include accurate metric information about physical arrays.

The manipulation of mental imagery

The findings of the experiments on mental scanning that I have just discussed suggest that the spatial relationships between the objects in an imaged array correspond to the relationships which would hold between the same objects in a physical array. A further issue is whether the way in which imaged objects can be manipulated corresponds to the way in which actual physical objects might be manipulated.

As I mentioned above, some tests of spatial ability seem to involve a process of mental rotation, and this was examined in detail by Shepard and Metzler (1971). They presented their subjects with computer-generated drawings showing perspective views of possible objects that could be constructed by joining together 10 identical cubical blocks (see Figure 3.1). Pairs of drawings were presented that showed (a) the same object, possibly viewed at different orientations in two-dimensional space, (b) the same object, possibly viewed from different perspectives in three-dimensional space, or (c) an object and its mirror image.

Shepard and Metzler found that the time taken to match two different views of the same object was directly related to the angle

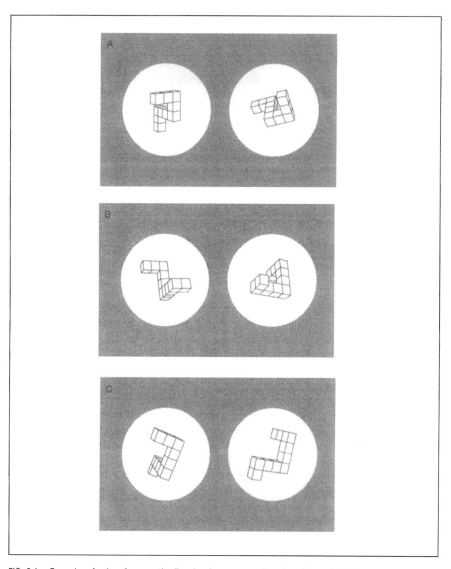

FIG. 3.1. Examples of pairs of perspective line drawings presented to the subjects. (A) A "same" pair, which differs by an 80° rotation in the picture plane; (B) a "same" pair, which differs by an 80° rotation in depth; and (C) a "different" pair, which cannot be brought into congruence by *any* rotation. Reprinted with permission from "Mental rotation of three-dimensional objects", by R.N. Shepard and J. Metzler, 1971, *Science, 171*, 702. Copyright © 1971 by the American Association for the Advancement of Science.

between the two views (which varied between 0° and 180°), and there was essentially no difference between objects rotated within the picture plane and those which were rotated in depth. This indicated that the subjects had been mentally rotating three-dimensional representations of one or both objects at a constant rate until they had the same orientation (at which point they could be judged to be the same or different by a simple matching process). All of the subjects reported using imagery in order to carry out this process of mental rotation.

The question arises whether one would obtain a similar pattern of performance when the subjects have to carry out a whole sequence of such manipulations. Shepard and Feng (1972) investigated this possibility by presenting patterns of six connected squares which would result when the faces of a cube were unfolded onto a flat surface. The subjects were asked to say whether two arrows marked on the edges of different squares would meet if the squares were folded back up into a cube. Some examples are shown in Figure 3.2;

FIG. 3.2. Mental paper-folding: six illustrative problems. From "A chronometric study of mental paper folding", by R.N. Shepard and C. Feng, 1972, *Cognitive Psychology*, *3*, 230. Copyright © 1972 by Academic Press, Inc. Reprinted with permission.

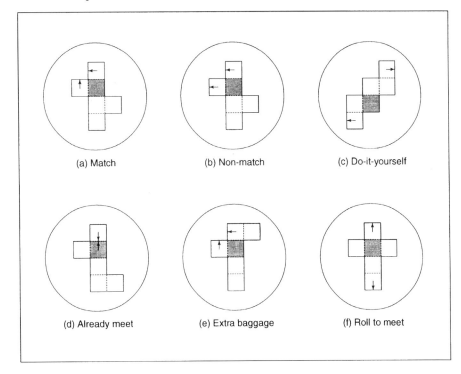

(a) Match

(b) Non-match

(c) Do-it-yourself

(d) Already meet

(e) Extra baggage

(f) Roll to meet

in each pattern, the shaded square represents the fixed base of the cube. Half the stimuli were "match" cases in which the two arrows would in fact meet (as in Panel A); the other half were "non-match" cases in which the two arrows could not be made to meet (as in Panel B). This, too, was based upon tasks included in tests of spatial ability.

Once again, all of the subjects reported using imagery to carry out the task: "Some Ss [subjects] described this imagery process as being primarily visual; others spoke, as well, of a strong kinesthetic component in which they imagined folding up the cube with their own hands" (p. 242). An initial inspection of the results indicated that the response time for the "match" cases varied with the number of individual folds that would have to be carried out to bring the arrows together if they were physically performed. For example, Panel C in Figure 3.2 needs a total of five different folds and was associated with longer response times. Shepard and Feng argued that even the simplest example where the arrows already met (Panel D) still required one fold to achieve a 90° angle between the squares.

On closer inspection, however, a much better predictor of response time was the sum of the number of squares that would be involved in each fold. Indeed, responses were slower even if there were additional squares that were not strictly relevant to the task of joining up the two arrows but merely constituted "extra baggage" (as in Panel E in Figure 3.2). Shepard and Feng argued that this was evidence against the notion that subjects were carrying out the task using some kind of verbal reasoning, because this would have ignored information that was extraneous to the physical relationship between the two arrows. Finally, the response times appeared to be faster if the arrows were at the opposite ends of a continuous string of four squares which could be "rolled up" in a single manoeuvre rather than in four separate folds (as in the case of Panel F).

A more complex task was devised by Cooper and Shepard (1973), in which the subjects were required to judge whether common alphanumeric characters were presented in their normal form or as mirror-image reversals. On each trial, the subject was instructed to construct a mental image of the appropriate character in one of six different orientations; the character was then presented either in that orientation or in one of the other five. The results showed that reaction time once again increased with the angular discrepancy between the anticipated orientation and the actual orientation of the character. From these results, Cooper and Shepard inferred that the subjects had rotated their visual images at a constant rate until they were at the same orientation as the test character. This interpretation of the results was once again borne out by the subjects' own reports concerning their use of mental imagery.

These results suggest that the way in which imaged objects can be manipulated corresponds to the way in which physical objects might be manipulated (see Shepard & Podgorny, 1978). Finke (1989) characterised this feature of mental imagery as the "principle of transformational equivalence":

> Imagined transformations and physical transformations exhibit corresponding dynamic characteristics and are governed by the same laws of motion. (p. 93)

Mental comparisons

A rather different experimental paradigm that was developed to compare the role of imagery and other mental representations involved the comparison of pairs of objects on some dimension when the objects themselves were presented in a symbolic form (for example, as their names or as pictures).

When people compare two actual objects on some physical dimension, such as size or area, their reaction times obey a reliable psychophysical function, such that responses are given more quickly, the greater the absolute difference between the two objects along the relevant dimension. Moyer (1973) asked whether a similar function would be found when subjects were comparing visual symbols that represented physical objects. Specifically, he presented his subjects with the names of two animals, such as *frog–wolf*, and asked them to indicate which was the name of the larger animal. He found that their response times decreased as the difference between the actual sizes of the animals increased. Moyer suggested that people compared named animals by making an "internal" psychophysical judgement after having converted the names into some analogue representation (that is, one which preserved information about actual physical size).

To the extent that similar results are obtained both from perceptual comparisons and from symbolic, mental comparisons, it might be suggested that the cognitive representation that is employed in mental comparisons was structurally equivalent to perceptual experience, as in the experiments on mental rotation described above. Paivio (1975b) made a more specific proposal: that mental comparisons were carried out on the basis of mental images of exemplars of the two concepts to be compared. His preliminary investigations included the use of questionnaires in which subjects reported the sorts of strategies employed in comparing the physical sizes of named objects, and the results "indicated an overwhelming reliance on visual imagery" (p. 637). Nevertheless, Paivio himself regarded this as only "supplementary evidence" that such a process was functionally activated" (p. 646).

The regular empirical function which Moyer (1973) obtained between response times and the magnitude of the difference between two named objects has been called the *symbolic distance effect*. An interesting variant of the mental comparison task was devised by Paivio (1978a), who asked subjects to compare clock times in terms of the angles between the hour and minute hands. For example, at which of the following times do the hour and minute hands form the smaller angle: 3:55 and 10:40? (See Figure 3.3.) Most subjects reported the use of imagery to solve this problem (that is, they compared the angles formed by the hands on visualised clock faces), and once again there was a reliable symbolic distance effect, so that the reaction times were longer with smaller angular differences.

Mental comparisons on more abstract, semantic dimensions appear to take longer than those on physical dimensions. What is perhaps more surprising is that mental comparisons on abstract dimensions reliably produce symbolic distance effects. Indeed, the earliest studies of mental comparisons had involved judgements of numerical magnitude when subjects were presented with pairs of

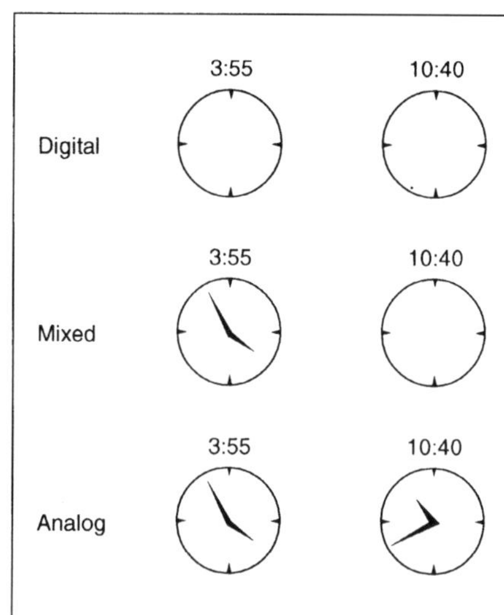

FIG. 3.3.
Examples of stimuli used by Paivio (1978a): a simple comparison of two digital times, a "mixed" comparison in which one digital time was accompanied by pictorial information in the form of an analogue clock, and an "analog" condition in which both digital times were accompanied by analogue clocks. From "Comparison of mental clocks", by A. Paivio, 1978, *Journal of Experimental Psychology: Human Perception and Performance, 4*, 67. Copyright © 1978 by the American Psychological Association. Reprinted with permission.

single digits. Symbolic distance effects have been found in judgements of the alphabetic ordering of pairs of letters and in comparisons of time (longer versus shorter), quality (better versus worse), temperature (warmer versus colder), the intelligence of animals, the military power of countries, and the monetary cost of cars (see J.T.E. Richardson, 1980b, p. 48). Finally, Friedman (1978) obtained a symbolic distance effect when subjects were asked to compare pairs of low-imagery words in terms of which made them feel better or worse.

However, the theoretical interest of the symbolic distance effect became even more questionable when it was demonstrated with non-semantic properties of words, as in judgements of the relative frequency with which words occur in everyday language, or judgements of the relative ease or difficulty with which words can be pronounced. The symbolic distance effect was also found when subjects made mental comparisons among items which they had learned in some totally arbitrary ordering. Since the effect seems to result from mental comparisons made along any ordered dimension whatsoever, it would not be informative as to the specific strategy or process used by subjects to carry out particular sorts of comparison (see J.T.E. Richardson, 1980b, p. 48).

An important alternative source of evidence regarding the nature of the representation used in mental comparisons was the comparison of performance when pictures and words were used as materials. A basic assumption of Paivio's (1975b) theoretical position, which will be discussed in more detail in Chapter 4, was that imagery should be evoked more readily by pictures of objects than by the names of objects. If, as Paivio maintained, mental comparisons were based on the use of imagery, it would follow that mental comparisons should be faster with pictures than with words as materials. The first investigation of this idea was carried out by Paivio (1975b), who asked subjects to compare concrete objects in terms of their physical size. Both pictures and words produced a symbolic distance effect, and, as he had predicted, reaction times were substantially faster with pictures than with words. Paivio (1978a) obtained very similar results when people were asked to compare clock times. However, in this task the pictorial materials directly represented the relevant information (the angular separation of the hands), and so the pictorial comparison was reduced to a visual comparison involving pairs of analogue clocks (see Figure 3.3).

Paivio (1975b) also assessed performance using pictorial presentation when the pictured sizes of the two objects were incongruent with their actual size. In this case, subjects had to respond "larger" to the picture that was physically smaller. Under these circumstances, reaction times were slower than with congruent pictorial presentations. Moreover, pairs of pictured objects which are incongruent with respect to their relative size are *congruent* with respect to their apparent relative distance. In accordance with this idea, Paivio found that these pairs produced faster reaction times when the subjects were asked to make judgements of apparent distance. However, although these experiments showed that mental comparisons could be speeded or slowed by congruent or incongruent perceptual information, they did not show that these comparisons were made on the basis of representations that preserved such information in a specifically analogical or imagistic fashion.

The superiority of pictorial presentation over verbal presentation is consistent with the idea that mental imagery is involved in mental comparisons between concrete objects on the basis of physical attributes. However, other research showed that pictorial presentation was superior to verbal presentation in the case of judgements of the intelligence of animals, and Paivio (1978c) himself obtained similar results in judgements concerning pleasantness or monetary value. He suggested that properties such as intelligence, pleasantness, and value should be regarded as attributes of things rather than words, and that it was necessary to produce images of the things in question in order to make comparisons with respect to these properties.

Support for the latter notion was obtained by comparing performance on pictures and words in judgements of non-semantic properties of words. For example, Paivio (1975b) showed that mental comparisons of the pronounceability of object names were slower when the objects were pictured than when their names were visually presented. Similar results were obtained in other studies when subjects compared the relative frequency with which object names occurred in everyday language. Paivio concluded that these sorts of mental comparisons were not made with the help of mental imagery.

A third category of evidence concerning the nature of the representations used in mental comparisons comes from the investigation of individual differences in the use of imagery. In research on mental comparisons, this approach was based on tests of spatial ability. Evidence was obtained to show that subjects of high spatial ability carried out mental comparisons of physical objects in terms of their size or shape faster than subjects of low spatial ability. Verbal ability proved to be unrelated to performance in these tasks (see J.T.E. Richardson, 1980b, p. 51). In his investigation of mental clocks, Paivio (1978a) obtained very similar findings; in particular, subjects of high spatial ability produced faster responses than subjects of low spatial ability in comparing the angular separation of the hands of imagined clocks at times expressed in a digital form, whereas verbal ability was not correlated with performance.

Paivio (1978c) provided evidence on individual differences with regard to mental comparisons based on abstract attributes. For comparisons of both pleasantness and monetary value, the response times of subjects of high spatial ability were significantly faster than those of subjects of low spatial ability. In neither case was the effect of verbal ability significant. These results supported Paivio's hypothesis that properties such as intelligence, pleasantness, and value were attributes of things rather than words, and consequently that even mental comparisons based upon abstract dimensions such as these were made using images of the named objects. Finally, Paivio referred to an unpublished study which found no sign of an effect of spatial ability upon mental comparisons regarding the relative familiarity of words. This supported the converse suggestion that mental comparisons on non-semantic dimensions of words were not made with the help of mental imagery.

In order to ensure the compatibility of these conclusions with phenomenal experience, I carried out an experiment where subjects performed a mental-comparison task and then completed a questionnaire on the strategies which they had used to carry out this task (J.T.E. Richardson, 1979c). The items to be compared were the names of animals, as in the original study by Moyer (1973). My subjects reported using imagery 73% of the time when making judgements on physical dimensions such as size or angularity, 79% of the time when making judgements on abstract dimensions such as ferocity or intelligence, but only 13% of the time when making judgements on non-semantic dimensions such as frequency and pronounceability. These results were entirely consistent with Paivio's account of mental comparisons, according to which objects were judged along both physical and abstract dimensions by the comparison of their mental images.

Visuo-spatial working memory

A rather different kind of experimental research has been based upon the idea that the representation of objects in the form of mental images is based upon the same cognitive mechanisms that are involved in the perception of those objects. Finke (1989) characterised this idea as the "principle of perceptual equivalence":

> Imagery is functionally equivalent to perception to the extent that similar mechanisms in the visual system are activated when objects or events are imagined as when the same objects or events are actually perceived. (p. 41)

One implication of this is that the maintenance of mental imagery can disrupt performance in perceptual tasks, especially in the detection of faint stimuli. This notion was extensively studied in a series of projects by Segal and her collaborators, and the major conclusions of this research are straightforward (see Segal, 1971). First, sensory sensitivity in detection experiments is reduced if the subjects are required to maintain mental images. Second, this reduction in sensory sensitivity is roughly twice as great if the signal and the mental image are in the same sensory modality than if they are in different modalities. For instance, auditory imagery interferes more with the detection of auditory signals, but visual imagery interferes more with the detection of visual signals. Thus, although there is a generalised effect of mental imagery upon perceptual sensitivity, there is a modality-specific effect, too. This is consistent with the idea of a functional overlap between imagery and perception, but Bower (1972) suggested that it could just reflect peripheral effects: for example, visual imagery might reduce visual sensitivity by producing pupillary dilation and misfocusing.

The converse implication is that some kinds of perceptual tasks might selectively interfere with one's ability to create and use mental images because they would be competing for the same cognitive resources. This idea was first raised by Brooks (1967), who studied the extent of competition or functional overlap between reading, listening, and imaging. In a typical experiment, Brooks asked his subjects to listen to messages describing the spatial relationship among digits placed within an imaginary matrix array. An example would be: "In the starting square put a 1. In the next square to the *right*, put a 2. In the next square *up* put a 3", and so on. Some of the messages were, in addition, presented visually in the form of a typewritten display. For comparison, control messages of the same form and length were presented in which the words *quick, slow, good,* and *bad* were substituted for the words *right, left, up,* and *down.* In each case, the subjects were asked to recall the message word for word immediately after it had been read out. For the control messages, hearing and reading a message produced better performance than hearing the message alone. However, the reverse was true for the spatial messages, which implied that reading selectively interfered with the mental representation of spatial information in the form of images.

Baddeley, Grant, Wight, and Thomson (1975) attempted to interfere with performance on Brooks's task by making their subjects track a moving visual target with a stylus while the sentences were being read out. They found that this disrupted the subsequent recall of the spatial messages but had no effect on the recall of the control messages. Baddeley and Lieberman (1980) attempted to separate the visual and spatial components of this disruption. They devised two different tasks to be carried out while the subjects were listening to the messages: a visual, non-spatial task in which the subject made successive brightness judgements; and a non-visual, spatial task in which the blindfolded subject tracked a moving pendulum with a flashlight using auditory feedback provided through a photocell and tone-generator attached to the pendulum. They found that the auditory-tracking task caused a much greater impairment on the spatial messages than on the control messages, but there was no such difference in the case of the brightness-judgement task.

Baddeley and Lieberman interpreted their findings in terms of the theory of "working memory" that had been put forward by Baddeley and Hitch (1974). To try to explain certain puzzling findings in the short-term recall of digits, letters, and words, Baddeley and Hitch proposed that this was based on a complex system which consisted of at least two components: a central executive processor and a subsidiary component specialised for holding verbal material (nowadays known as the "phonological loop"). The account of the latter component was subsequently refined in the light of further research in terms of a passive phonological store to which spoken messages could gain direct access and a control process involving the use of (either overt or covert) articulatory rehearsal to maintain or "refresh" the contents of the phonological store (see Baddeley, 1986).

Baddeley and Hitch had suggested that there might be other subsystems whose role was to support the central executive processor. In particular, they raised the idea of a peripheral memory component based on the visual system, and they described several tasks using visual perception or visual imagery that might be used to study its operation. Baddeley and Lieberman (1980) took their own findings to confirm the existence of this further component of working memory, which was described as a visuo-spatial "scratch pad" or "sketch-pad". The fact that this store appeared to be sensitive to disruption by concurrent movement and not by a concurrent visual task suggested that it was spatial in nature rather than specifically visual.

Other researchers have confirmed that visual short-term memory can be disrupted by concurrent irrelevant movements, but disruption by irrelevant visual materials (such as patterns or coloured patches) has also been found. These results suggest that visuo-spatial working memory involves a passive short-term store which has a direct link with the processes underlying visual perception, but which can be refreshed by a form of spatial rehearsal that can be blocked or suppressed by irrelevant movements (see Logie, 1995). This picture of visuo-spatial working memory is pleasingly symmetrical with current accounts of the phonological loop (see Figure 3.4).

This picture is nowadays widely accepted, at least as a framework for research. Nevertheless, it assumes that working memory constitutes a kind of "gateway" between sensory input and more permanent knowledge structures that are to be found in long-term memory. Logie (1995, pp. 126–128; 1996) argued instead that information must gain access to long-term memory before being processed within working memory. For example, the encoding of

FIG. 3.4.
A schematic diagram of the working memory model proposed by Baddeley (1986). From *Visuo-Spatial Working Memory* (p. 18), by R.H. Logie, 1995, Hove, UK: Lawrence Erlbaum Associates Ltd. Copyright © 1995 by Lawrence Erlbaum Associates Ltd. Reprinted by permission of Psychology Press, Hove, UK.

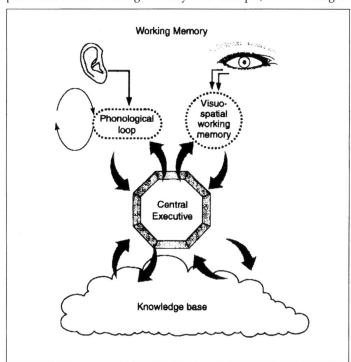

items within the phonological loop depends upon knowledge concerning the phonology and pronunciation of the person's native language, whereas the encoding of items within the visuo-spatial scratchpad depends upon knowledge concerning the appearance of physical objects. Consequently, the contents of both the passive phonological store and its visuo-spatial counterpart are interpreted representations that are derived from the activation of knowledge structures in long-term memory (see Figure 3.5).

In this revised model, the phenomenal experience of visual imagery is the result of central executive processes operating on the interpreted contents of the passive visual store within working memory (Logie, 1995, pp. 129–131). Evidence for a link between the subsidiary components of the working-memory system and the phenomenal experience of mental imagery was obtained by Baddeley

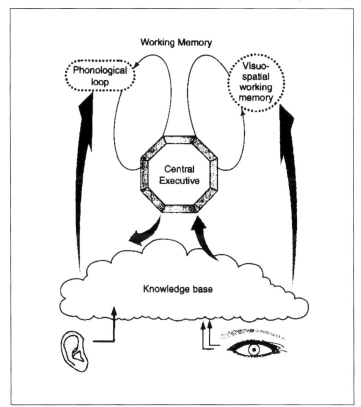

FIG. 3.5.
A schematic view of working memory as a workspace rather than a gateway for cognition. From *Working Memory and Human Cognition* (p. 56), by J.T.E. Richardson, R.W. Engle, L. Hasher, R.H. Logie, E.R. Stoltzfus, and R.T. Zacks, 1996, New York: Oxford University Press. Copyright © 1996. Used by permission of Oxford University Press, Inc.

and Andrade (1998). They found that subjects gave lower ratings of the vividness of a visual image when they were required to carry out a concurrent visual or spatial task, but they gave lower ratings of the vividness of an auditory image when they were required to carry out a concurrent articulatory task. The same results were obtained regardless of whether the images in question originated in information that had recently been perceived or information retrieved from long-term memory.

Image and Mind

A quite similar account is to be found in the theory that was put forward by Kosslyn (1980) in his book, *Image and Mind*. This had originally been developed in the light of the results obtained in the image-scanning experiments mentioned in the previous chapter, as well as purely logical analyses of what might be involved in constructing and manipulating images. Nevertheless, it was also intended to handle the findings obtained by Shepard and his colleagues on the rotation and transformation of mental images and to address a number of conceptual problems that had been raised about the validity of imagery as an explanatory construct in experimental psychology.

Kosslyn argued that an image consisted of two components. On the one hand, there was a "surface" representation: in other words, a quasi-pictorial entity held within some form of active memory. It was this component which was apparently accompanied by the subjective experience of having a mental image. On the other hand, there was a "deep" representation: in other words, the information stored within long-term memory from which the surface representation was derived (p. 139).

According to Kosslyn, the surface representation was held in a visual buffer in which spatial arrays were constructed and transformed as the result of complex processes operating upon the information stored within long-term memory. These arrays were represented as configuration of points in a matrix, which Kosslyn likened to displays on a computer's display screen (pp. 6–8, 135–136). However, unlike computer displays, images were most vivid and sharply defined near the centre of the display, so that the visual buffer mimicked the contrast between central and peripheral vision in human perception (p. 140).

There were two kinds of deep representations. Both were represented in an abstract form which Kosslyn likened to files held on a computer's disk storage device:

1. One kind of representation contained encoded information about the literal or perceptual appearance of objects. This information was represented by lists that specified which cells in the visual buffer should be filled. In Kosslyn's model, these files were identified by the extension IMG (for instance, "CAR.IMG").
2. The second kind of representation contained information about the appearance of objects expressed in a discursive or propositional format. In the model, these files were identified by the extension PRP (for instance, "CAR.PRP"). These consisted of lists of propositions which described the parts of an object or a scene, the location of a part on an object or of an object in a scene, the approximate size of an object or a part, the critical aspects of an object's appearance, the superordinate category to which the object belonged, the names of other files containing a literal representation of the object's appearance, and the spatial relations among various objects (pp. 142–146).

Kosslyn went on to specify in detail the processes that would be needed for generating, evaluating, and transforming images according to this model. The most important of these are described in Box 3.3, and Figure 3.6 shows how the structures postulated by Kosslyn's

Box 3.3.   Outline of the theory-relevant processes in Kosslyn's (1980) model. Reprinted by permission of the publisher from *Image and Mind* (pp. 150–151), by S.M. Kosslyn, Cambridge, MA: Harvard University Press. Copyright © 1980 by the President and Fellows of Harvard College.

Name	Type[1]	Input[2]	Operation	Output
PICTURE	P	r, θ file [size, location, orientation]	Maps points into surface matrix; mapping function may be adjusted to vary size, location, and/or orientation.	Configuration of points depicting contents of an IMG file (produces new format; if mapping function adjusted also produces new content).
FIND	C	Name of sought part	Looks up description; looks up procedures specified in description; executes procedures on surface matrix.	Passes back Locate/Not Locate; if Locate, passes back Cartesian coordinates of part.
PUT	P	Name of to-be-placed part	Looks up name of image file, location relation, and foundation part; looks up description of foundation part and relation; calls FIND to locate foundation part; adjusts mapping function; calls PICTURE.	Part integrated into image (produces new content). (Cont'd overleaf)

Box 3.3 cont'd

Name	Type[1]	Input[2]	Operation	Output
IMAGE	P	Name of to-be-imaged object(s) [size, location, orientation, level of detail]	Locates IMG file; calls PICTURE [if size, location, or orientation specified, adjusts mapping function; if detail required, searches for HASA entries, calls PUT].	Detailed or skeletal image at specified or default size, location, and/or orientation (produces new content with different format, organization).
RESOLUTION	P	Surface image	Computes density of points in image.	A number indicating dot density of image (produces new format).
REGENERATE	A	Surface image	Works over surface matrix, refreshing most-faded parts first until all parts are refreshed.	Image reactivated, with sharpness relations among parts altered (alters content).
LOOKFOR	P	Command to find a named part or property on an image	Calls REGENERATE; looks up description and size of part; calls RESOLUTION; if density not optimal, calls ZOOM or PAN; checks whether image overflows in direction of part, if so calls SCAN; calls FIND; if part not located searches for relevant HASA entries, calls PUT to insert regions, calls FIND.	Found/Not Found response.
SCAN	A	Image, direction of required shift [rate]	Moves all points in surface matrix along vector; fills in new material at leading edge via inverse mapping function.	Image repositioned (alters content).
ZOOM	A	Surface image, target resolution [rate]	Moves all points in surface matrix out from the center; fills in new material via inverse mapping function; calls RESOLUTION; calls PUT to insert new parts as resolution allows.	Scale change in image, higher resolution, and new parts (alters content).
PAN	A	Surface image, target resolution [rate]	Moves all points in surface matrix in from the center.	Scale change in image, lower resolution (alters content).
ROTATE	A	Image, angle, and direction [rate]	Moves all points in bounded region in specified direction around a pivot.	Reorients image (alters content).

1. A indicates alteration transformations, which alter the initial data-structure; P indicates production transformations, which do not alter the initial data-structure but produce a new one from it; C indicates comparison operations, which compare two data-structures or parts thereof.
2. Optional input is indicated in brackets.

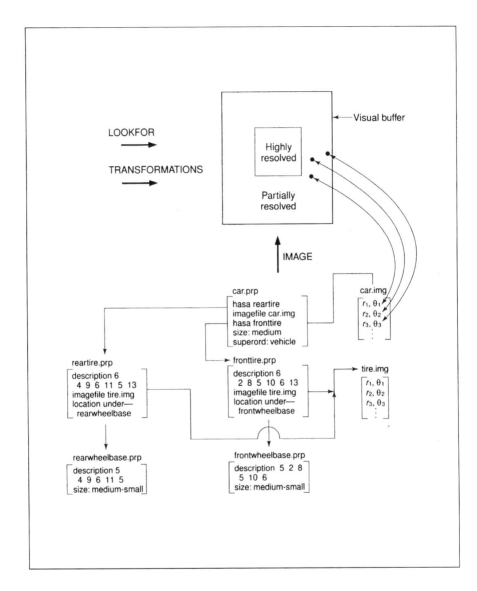

FIG. 3.6. A schematic representation of the structures and processes posited by Kosslyn's (1980) theory. The words in large type indicate the major classes of processes and the locus of their action. Reprinted by permission of the publisher from *Image and Mind* (p. 147), by S.M. Kosslyn, Cambridge, MA: Harvard University Press. Copyright © 1980 by the President and Fellows of Harvard College.

theory would be combined to generate a visual image (in this case, of a car). PICTURE created a new configuration in the visual buffer depicting the contents of a description in long-term visual memory; FIND identified the location of a named part in the visual buffer; PUT integrated the named part into the existing image; and IMAGE created the image of a named object by coordinating three other procedures.

The remaining processes were involved in the inspection or transformation of images. RESOLUTION was used to decide whether it was necessary either to "zoom in" or to "pan out" to locate a named part or property of an object. REGENERATE refreshed and sharpened the existing image, and LOOKFOR searched for a named part or property within the existing image. SCAN repositioned the image by means of a linear transformation. ZOOM increased the resolution of an image (inserting new parts if necessary), PAN reduced the resolution of the image, and finally ROTATE reorientated the image to reveal previously obscured parts.

One important property of Kosslyn's theory is that information about physical objects could be accessed not only in the form of imagery but also in the form of propositional information. Consequently, in answering a question about the appearance of physical objects, there would be a "race" between the imaginal and propositional processes to arrive at the correct solution, and the person's observable behaviour would depend upon which won the race.

Kosslyn demonstrated this idea using the example of mental comparisons (pp. 351–363). As I mentioned earlier, when people compare two named objects on the basis of their physical size, there is typically a symbolic distance effect (their response times decrease as the differences between the actual sizes of the objects increase). This has been taken as evidence for the use of mental imagery in size comparisons. However, Kosslyn showed that, when people had learned to identify the objects in question as "large" or "small" and had become highly practised at retrieving this information, there might be no symbolic distance effect for pairs of items from different categories. In this situation, they were able to access the categorical information more quickly than they could access the relevant perceptual information.

On Kosslyn's account, the precise contribution of mental imagery to objective performance in any particular task depends upon the processing components that are being tapped by that task. Moreover, the parameters determining the efficiency of these processing components are quantities that in principle can vary across different individuals. Kosslyn, Brunn, Cave, and Wallach (1984) successfully validated this componential analysis against the patterns of performance produced by 50 subjects on a battery of tasks requiring different operations to be carried out on images of particular materials. However, Poltrock and Brown (1984) maintained that they could identify a single trait representing spatial visualisation ability which was measured by performance on a battery of laboratory tasks involving imagery and which in turn predicted performance on tests of spatial visualisation. Subsequently, Kosslyn, Van Kleeck, and Kirby (1990) revised Kosslyn's theory to take into account neuroanatomical and neurophysiological findings, and they found that it then achieved an even better fit to the pattern of correlations among individual test scores than had been obtained by Kosslyn et al. (1984).

Images and propositions

Nevertheless, Kosslyn's (1980) model attracted a fair amount of sceptical criticism, mainly motivated by an earlier article by Pylyshyn (1973), who had argued that imagery could not function as an explanatory construct in psychological theories of cognition, and that imagery phenomena needed to be explained in terms of an underlying representational format based upon abstract propositions. Kosslyn and Pomerantz (1977) evaluated Pylyshyn's arguments in the light of the available evidence, and they concluded that

> there are no convincing arguments that images are not represented in a distinct format, nor can imagery phenomena be easily accounted for by appealing to propositional representations. In addition, there is some evidence that emergent properties of images do in fact play a functional role in cognition. (p. 74)

J.R. Anderson (1978) considered the evidence discussed by Kosslyn and Pomerantz (1977), and he concluded that in each case what had been taken as evidence for a particular kind of representation (namely, imagery) was actually evidence for a possible process operating upon the representation, where there was no good reason to associate the relevant process with that particular representation. The crux of Anderson's paper was that this is a general problem that has to be faced in deciding among different theoretical positions in any area of cognitive psychology:

It is not possible for behavioral data to uniquely decide issues of internal representation. The reason is that one cannot just test questions about a representation in the abstract. One must perform tests of the representation in combination with certain assumptions about the processes that use the representation. That is, one must test a representation–process pair. One can show that given a set of assumptions about an image representation and a set of processes that operate on it, one can construct an equivalent set of assumptions about a propositional representation and its processes. Or one can be given a propositional theory and construct an equivalent imagery theory. In fact, it is possible to establish a more general claim: Given any representation–process pair it is possible to construct other pairs with different representations whose behavior is equivalent to it. These pairs make up for differences in representation by assuming compensating differences in the processes. (pp. 262–263)

Thus, Anderson was arguing that it is not possible to decide between theories postulating imaginal and propositional representations strictly on the basis of behavioural data. Anderson considered various alternative, non-behavioural criteria for deciding among hypothesised representations. Most of these were formal criteria (that is, ones to do with the logical structure of the proposed representations); these included parsimony, plausibility, efficiency, and optimality. Such criteria relate to the manner in which rival theories describe the research findings which have actually been obtained. Only one of the sets of criteria put forward by Anderson was substantive, in the sense that it is relevant to determining whether a theory correctly describes the operation of the underlying psychological mechanisms. These criteria involve the use of physiological data and neuropsychological research to establish the localisation of the hypothesised functions within the brain.

Anderson considered that none of these alternative criteria was of much use in trying to discriminate among different theories of cognitive representation, and he therefore concluded that no one theory could give rise to a unique set of empirical predictions. However, most cognitive psychologists would find this position unpalatable. Instead, they would argue that the role of psychological theories is to specify the mechanisms and processes which underlie cognitive abilities, and that these mechanisms and processes are in principle to be discovered amongst the physiological structures of the central nervous system. As a consequence, physiological data and neuropsychological research will be of immense value when trying to discriminate among alternative theories. What does this research have to say about the use of mental imagery as an internal representation?

Imagery and the brain

Damage to the posterior regions of the brain, and especially to the parietal lobes of the cerebral cortex, tends to produce impaired performance on tests of spatial thinking. Although such deficits may result from damage to either side of the brain, they are more likely following damage to the right cerebral hemisphere. However, the relative frequency of deficits in patients with damage to the right hemisphere varies from task to task. Thus, it would appear that physiological mechanisms in both hemispheres may contribute to visuo-spatial working memory, but different tasks may make different requirements of the components in the two parietal lobes (see J.T.E. Richardson, 1980b, p. 135).

De Renzi and Nichelli (1975) described several patients whose long-term visuo-spatial memory (as evidenced by informal observation as well as by their performance on a test of maze learning) was essentially normal but whose short-term visuo-spatial memory (as evidenced from a spatial analogue of the test of digit span) was severely impaired. Within this sample, different patients had lesions within both hemispheres. Two of these patients were notable insofar as their verbal short-term memory was essentially intact. De Renzi and Nichelli presented two other patients with a selective impairment of verbal short-term memory but intact visuo-spatial short-term memory. Taken together, these findings imply that the mechanisms responsible for verbal and visuo-spatial working memory are functionally dissociable.

Early investigations involving electroencephalographic measurements in experimental tasks thought to involve imagery produced very little consistent evidence for any differential hemispheric involvement (see Ehrlichman & Barrett, 1983). Clearer evidence on the cerebral localisation of different aspects of imagery comes from the study of regional cerebral blood flow. Roland and Friberg (1985) examined the pattern of brain activity when people were visualising a walk through their own neighbourhood, and they found increased activation in the frontal, superior occipital, posterior inferior temporal, and posterior superior parietal regions of both hemispheres.

Goldenberg, Podreka, Steiner, Suess, Deecke, and Willmes (1988) compared the patterns of blood flow when people judged as either true or false general-knowledge statements about the appearance of physical objects (sentences such as "The green of pine trees is darker than that of grass" and "The letter W consists of three straight lines") and statements about abstract concepts (sentences such as "Columbus named the natives of America *Indians* because he believed he was in India" and "the categorical imperative is an ancient grammatical form"). Although there was no difference between these conditions in terms of the overall activity of the two cerebral hemispheres, there was an increase in the activation of the left inferior occipital lobe when the subjects were judging statements about physical objects. Intriguingly, a patient described by Farah, Levine, and Calvanio (1988) who showed a "mental imagery deficit" following an infarction of the left posterior cerebral artery exhibited a selective impairment on this set of sentences when given this task.

Deutsch, Bourbon, Papanicolaou, and Eisenberg (1988) measured changes in regional cerebral blood flow whilst 19 subjects were carrying out the mental-rotation task devised by Shepard and Metzler (1971). They found an increase in cerebral blood flow within the parietal and occipital lobes of both hemispheres and also in the right frontal lobe. Williams, Rippon, Stone, and Annett (1995) measured EEG activity at 14 different locations across the scalp while 20 subjects were carrying out a similar task. They found suppression of the alpha rhythm (which implies increased brain activity) in the parietal regions of both hemispheres and in the left frontal region. Subsequently, M.S. Cohen et al. (1996) used functional MRI to monitor cortical activity while 10 subjects were carrying out Shepard and Metzler's task. They too found an increased level of activation in both cerebral hemispheres, which arose mainly within the superior parietal and frontal regions.

On the basis of experiments with animals, Ungerleider and Mishkin (1982) argued that two different cortical systems were involved in visual perception: the ventral (or anterior) system was specialised for object perception (identifying *what* an object is) and was located in the inferior temporal lobes; but the dorsal (or posterior) system was specialised for spatial perception (locating *where* an object is) and was located in the posterior parietal lobes. These two systems are illustrated in Figure 3.7 by reference to the brain of the rhesus monkey and a number of specific anatomical

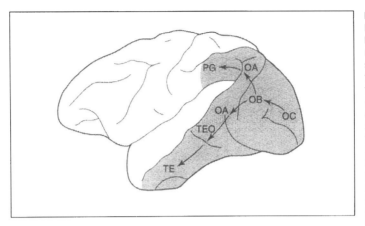

FIG. 3.7.
Lateral view of the
left hemisphere of a
rhesus monkey. The
shaded area defines
the cortical visual
tissue in the
occipital, temporal,
and parietal lobes.
Arrows schematise
two cortical
pathways, each
beginning in the
primary visual
cortex (area OC),
diverging within
prestriate cortex
(areas OB and OA),
and then coursing
either ventrally into
the inferior temporal
cortex (areas TEO
and TE) or dorsally
into the inferior
parietal cortex (area
PG). Both cortical
pathways are crucial
for higher visual
function, the ventral
pathway for object
vision and the
dorsal pathway for
spatial vision. From
"Object vision and
spatial vision: Two
cortical pathways",
by M. Mishkin,
L.G. Ungerleider,
and K.A. Macko,
1983, *Trends in
Neurosciences, 6,*
414. Reprinted with
permission.

regions of the cerebral cortex that were defined by Bonin and Bailey (1947).

Levine, Warach, and Farah (1985) proposed that these two systems (which they called the "what" system and the "where" system, respectively) were also involved in mental imagery. From a review of the clinical literature and the detailed study of two individual cases, they identified two distinct groups of patients. One group, who typically had received bilateral damage in the temporal–occipital cortex, had difficulties in recognising faces and colours, and they had analogous problems when using imagery to describe objects from memory. The other group, who typically had received bilateral damage in the parietal–occipital cortex, had difficulties in visual orientation and analogous problems in using imagery to describe directions and spatial relations. Levine et al. concluded that imagery for objects and colours could be dissociated from imagery for spatial relations (see also Farah, Hammond, Levine, & Calvanio, 1988).

In addition to these "ventral" and "dorsal" systems, Kosslyn et al. (1993) raised the idea that visual imagery might even involve the primary visual cortex (area OC in Figure 3.7), which is responsible for the initial analysis of perceptual information. They used positron emission tomography to measure regional cerebral blood flow whilst subjects were carrying out imaging tasks and found evidence for activation of some regions in the primary visual cortex. However, Mellet, Tzourio, Denis, and Mazoyer (1995) argued that these results were contaminated by artefacts in Kosslyn et al.'s procedure and open to other interpretations. In fact, the experiment by M.S. Cohen et al. (1996) which used functional MRI to monitor brain activity in

Shepard and Metzler's (1971) mental-rotation task found no evidence for increased activation within the primary visual cortex.

It is interesting that Finke (1989) arrived at essentially the same conclusion, purely on the basis of a critical review of the evidence obtained from experimental research concerning the visual characteristics of mental images and the degree of overlap between visual imagery and visual perception. With regard to the "principle of perceptual equivalence" which I quoted earlier in this chapter, Finke concluded:

> The principle of perceptual equivalence is supported by these findings, but there are limitations on how far down in the visual system the principle applies. Mental imagery does not seem to involve retinal or precortical levels of the visual system. . . . Nor does it seem likely that imagery involves the initial stages of information processing in the visual cortex, where simple feature analysis takes place. Rather, the principle appears to hold only down to levels in the visual system where visual associations occur. (p. 58)

Most research on the brain mechanisms that underlie mental imagery has been specifically concerned with visual imagery and not with imagery in other modalities. There is however evidence that broadly the same principles apply to imagery for movement. In particular, the measurement of regional cerebral blood flow has shown that imagining oneself to be performing an action is associated with increased activation in the brain regions that are involved in the control of actual movements (Decety, 1996). This in turn helps to explain why mental practice (that is, the imagined rehearsal of a particular action) enhances performance in many sporting activities (see Decety & Ingvar, 1990).

Imagery in "split-brain" patients

The computational approach developed by Kosslyn et al. (1984) has been applied in a particularly interesting way to the study of commissurotomy patients. Farah, Gazzaniga, Holtzman, and Kosslyn (1985) asked one such patient to classify individual lower-case letters of the alphabet according to their height. When the letters were briefly presented in their lower-case form to either side of the point of fixation, this patient achieved 100% accuracy for those letters presented to the right visual hemifield (and thus to the left hemisphere) and 90% accuracy for those letters presented to the left visual hemifield (and thus to the right hemisphere). However, when the letters were presented in their upper-case form and the subject was instructed to generate a mental image of their lower-case forms, his performance was 97% correct for those letters presented to the right visual hemifield, but only 43% correct (in other words, less than chance responding) for those presented to the left visual hemifield. In short, this patient was apparently unable to generate images of lower-case letters from upper-case letters presented to the right hemisphere, whereas this task was easily accomplished when the letters were presented to the left hemisphere. These results were taken to confirm Farah's (1984) hypothesis of a left-hemisphere locus for image generation.

A much more extensive investigation of this patient's performance was presented by Kosslyn, Holtzman, Farah, and Gazzaniga (1985). First, he was asked to classify individual upper-case letters according to whether or not they contained curved lines. When the letters were briefly presented in their upper-case form to either side of the point of fixation, he achieved 100% accuracy for those letters presented to the right visual hemifield and 97.5% accuracy for those presented to the left visual hemifield. However, when the same letters were presented in their lower-case form, his performance was still 100% correct for those letters presented to the right visual hemifield, but was markedly worse for those presented to the left visual hemifield (between 55% and 70% correct in different experiments). When the letters were presented auditorily and the patient responded by pointing to one of two locations, both situated to one side or the other of the point of fixation, he still achieved 95% accuracy when the locations were to the right of fixation, but his performance was at chance level (52% correct) when they were to the left of fixation. Subsequent experiments confirmed that this patient's right hemisphere was impaired in generating images of letters of the alphabet, and that this impairment could be overcome only by memorising the correct response to be given to each letter on the basis of feedback or by motor rehearsal of drawn shapes.

Nevertheless, Kosslyn et al. went on to demonstrate that there was no difference between this patient's left and right hemispheres with regard to his ability to answer questions about the global size and shape of physical objects when briefly presented with their names. When he was required to access information about the arrangement of particular details of these objects, however, a clear hemispheric asymmetry once again emerged, and performance on items presented to the left visual hemifield was at chance level. These findings were used to refine the earlier ideas into the notion of a left-hemisphere module specifically responsible for integrating the parts of an imaged object into the correct configuration. In contrast, the modules for activating information about physical objects that is stored within long-term visual memory and for identifying spatial patterns amongst the parts of an object appeared to be bilaterally represented.

A left-hemisphere advantage for the accuracy of image generation was broadly confirmed by Corballis and Sergent (1988, 1989) in testing another commissurotomised patient. This patient showed evidence of some residual capacity for image generation to items in the left visual hemifield when required to generate images of lower-case letters from their upper-case forms, although not when required to imagine the positions of hands on a clock face corresponding to digitally presented times. Moreover, in both cases the patient was *faster* at responding to items in the left visual hemifield than to items in the right visual hemifield. Corballis and Sergent then carried out a number of studies requiring their subject to judge whether letters rotated from their usual orientation were presented in their normal or mirror-imaged form. Normal subjects tend to show no differences in either speed or accuracy between the two hemifields in this task (W. Cohen & Polich, 1989; Corballis, 1982), which suggests a bilateral representation of the relevant neural mechanisms. However, this patient showed markedly superior performance in terms of both speed and accuracy when the items were presented in the left visual hemifield. Indeed, in the earlier testing sessions his performance was at chance level when items were presented in the right hemifield. Although some improvement was evident in the later sessions, the strong right-hemisphere advantage was essentially unaltered.

According to the model developed by Kosslyn (1980), mental-rotation tasks depend upon processes that transform a mental image, and the latter findings confirm the dissociation of such processes from those responsible for image generation. Nevertheless, Sergent (1990) emphasised that there was great variability among different split-brain patients, and that in any case they were not a representative sample of the general population. Indeed, other commissurotomised patients seem to have difficulty in carrying out mental rotation even when the items are presented centrally (Prigatano, Fordyce, Zeiner, Roueche, Pepping, & Wood, 1986, p. 620).

In the case of patients with focal brain lesions, one study appeared to suggest that mental rotation depended upon the integrity of the posterior regions of the right cerebral hemisphere (Ratcliff, 1979). However, other studies have found deficits on mental rotation following damage to either the left hemisphere or the right hemisphere (see Farah, 1989). Grossi, Modafferi, Pelosi, and Trojano (1989) described a patient with damage in the left occipito-temporal region who performed at chance level on the mental comparison of clock faces (the same task that was discussed earlier in this chapter), in spite of the fact that he had achieved a high level of accuracy on the perceptual version of this task. The study by Deutsch et al. (1988) of cerebral blood flow during mental rotation found statistically significant asymmetries across a group of 19 subjects; these indicated a higher level of activation in the right hemisphere than in the left hemisphere, especially in the frontal and parietal lobes. However, using functional MRI, M.S. Cohen et al. (1996) obtained no evidence for any consistent hemispheric lateralisation across another group of 10 subjects on this task. They did find that there was considerable individual variability in this regard, which suggests that the results obtained by Deutsch et al. may have been due to their fortuitous selection of an unrepresentative sample of subjects.

Imagery in unilateral neglect

The involvement of mental imagery as a cognitive representation has also been suggested in the case of the clinical symptom of unilateral neglect (which is also described as "visual neglect" or "hemi-neglect"). This is a tendency on the part of patients with damage to one side of the brain (typically resulting from strokes or tumours) to ignore objects and features within their immediate environment on the opposite side to their lesion. It is most commonly seen in patients with lesions of the parietal lobe, but it can also be found in patients with damage in other cortical regions or with lesions confined to the subcortex (see Vallar, 1993). Patients with damage to the left parietal lobe occasionally show neglect for their right-hand side, but visual neglect occurs most frequently and in its most severe and most persistent form after damage involving the right parietal lobe (Friedland & Weinstein, 1977). Neglect can be most easily shown in perceptual tasks such as line cancellation, where patients are instructed to inspect a visual display and to cross out all instances of a predesignated target (see Figure 3.8). However, it can sometimes

FIG. 3.8. A cancellation test (Albert, 1973) completed by a 62-year-old man after a right-hemisphere stroke. The central line was cancelled by the examiner as a demonstration, and the test was concluded when the subject said that all of the lines had been cancelled. From "The bisected image? Visual memory in patients with visual neglect" (p. 336), by A. Sunderland, 1990, in P.J. Hampson, D.F. Marks, & J.T.E. Richardson (Eds), *Imagery: Current Developments* (pp. 333–350), London: Routledge. Reprinted with permission.

also be seen in representational tasks, as in drawing a familiar object (such as a clock face or a square) from memory (see Figure 3.9).

Bisiach and Luzzatti (1978) asked two such patients to describe a scene that was familiar to them from before their illness, the Piazza del Duomo in Milan. When asked to imagine that they were facing the cathedral on the opposite side of the square, both patients described features that would have been to their right from this viewpoint but not those that would have been to their left. However, when asked to imagine that they were standing just in front of the cathedral and facing in the opposite direction, they described features that they had previously omitted, and they omitted the features that they had previously described.

Similar findings have been obtained in regard to people's knowledge about familiar geographical locations. For instance, Marshall, Halligan, and Robertson (1993) asked a patient with visual neglect to imagine that she was taking a walk from the south coast of England to the Highlands of Scotland (i.e. in a northerly direction) and to report the different towns that she would pass through. She

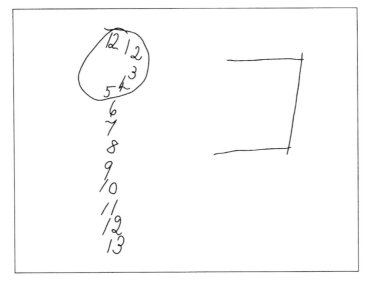

FIG. 3.9.
A "clock face" and a "square" drawn from memory by patients with severe visual neglect. From "The bisected image? Visual memory in patients with visual neglect" (p. 337), by A. Sunderland, 1990, in P.J. Hampson, D.F. Marks, & J.T.E. Richardson (Eds), *Imagery: Current Developments* (pp. 333–350), London: Routledge. Reprinted with permission.

described a series of locations on the east coast of Britain. However, when she was then asked to imagine taking a walk from Scotland to England (i.e. in a southerly direction), she listed a series of locations on the west coast of Britain that she had not mentioned previously.

Since these tasks concerned knowledge that would have been acquired before the onset of the brain damage that gave rise to visual neglect, it can be assumed that the patients' impairment in these tasks was not simply the result of perceptual deficits (see Beschin, Cocchini, Della Sala, & Logie, 1997). Bisiach and Luzzatti (1978) inferred from their results that visual neglect arose from the failure to form a representation of one side of external space (see also Barbut & Gazzaniga, 1987; Goldenberg, 1989). Consistent with this idea, Grossi et al. (1989) reported a patient with visual neglect who performed at chance level on both the perceptual comparison and mental comparison of clocks when the hands were on the left-hand side of the clock faces.

Bisiach, Luzzatti, and Perani (1979) attempted to test their hypothesis by forcing patients with unilateral neglect to construct representations from an immediate visual input. The subjects viewed cloud-like shapes passing in a horizontal plane behind a narrow vertical slit or aperture; their task was to say whether two successive shapes were the same or different. These patients detected 43% of pairs that differed on their right-hand side, but only 33% of pairs that differed on their left-hand side. Since all the information about the shapes themselves had come from the same central locus within the visual field, Bisiach et al. argued that this relative neglect could not be attributed to perceptual or attentional factors, but must instead reflect a selective impairment in constructing the left side of spatial images.

Similar results were obtained by Ogden (1985), who also found evidence for right-sided neglect among patients with left-sided damage in this task. However, Sunderland (1990) pointed out that in both of these studies the patients had already been exposed to the shapes in full view during an initial "static" condition in which the brain-damaged patients showed substantial levels of unilateral neglect. This procedure had been adopted in order to familiarise the subjects with the materials and procedure; even so, only half of Ogden's brain-damaged patients had been able to carry out the subsequent "dynamic" condition involving aperture viewing. Sunderland claimed that prior exposure to the shapes would probably have influenced the subjects' performance in the "dynamic" condition and that any residual neglect could be attributed to purely visual deficits.

As an alternative explanation of unilateral neglect, Sunderland suggested that the phenomenon could be seen as a deficit in the control of attention or spatial orientation. First, he noted that the scene-description effect originally described by Bisiach and Luzzatti (1978) was in fact contingent upon the experimental procedure. Bisiach, Capitani, Luzzatti, and Perani (1981) replicated the effect with a larger group of patients with damage to the right hemisphere, but, when these subjects were specifically asked to describe either the left side or the right side of the scene, there was no difference in the numbers of features that they recalled. Similarly, Mesulam (1985) described a patient with neglect whose performance in a cancellation task showed a marked improvement if he was given a cent for each accurate detection, and Meador, Loring, Bowers, and Heilman (1987) described a patient whose recall of features on the left side of an imagined scene improved if he was tested with his head and his eyes turned towards the left-hand side.

Second, the analysis that was proposed by Bisiach and his colleagues implied that brain-damaged patients ought to show neglect for one side of a single imagined object. Sunderland therefore asked 33 such patients to decide to which number the minute hand of a clock would point at different times to or past the hour. Twelve of the patients were unable to perform the task, and the remainder were compared with a control group of 30 normal subjects. The response times of all the subjects were generally slower for numbers on the left-hand side of the clock face, but there was no evidence that the brain-damaged patients were disproportionately slower on these numbers. In addition, there was no evidence of any relation between the extent of visual neglect according to a standard clinical test and the difference between the average response times for left-sided and right-sided numbers.

Finally, Sunderland reported a case study in which mental rotation was used to dissociate object-centred and ego-centred effects. A patient with visual neglect was asked to judge the position of an hour hand on a clock face containing just the number "12" that was rotated by 90° in either direction from the normal orientation. The response times for clock positions in his left hemispace were significantly longer than those for positions in his right hemispace; but the response times for positions on the clock's left hemi-face were (non-significantly) *faster* than those for positions on its right hemi-face.

In short:

- Patients with left-sided neglect seem to have no difficulty in recalling features from the left-hand side of an imagined scene once their attention has been directed towards those features.
- While patients with visual neglect are notoriously bad at drawing the left-hand side of a clock face, they show no evidence of neglect when their attention is directed to one side of an imagined clock face.
- Moreover, patients with left-sided neglect show no evidence of a selective loss of knowledge about the positions of numbers on the left side of a clock face, but they show a selective difficulty with positions in the left side of egocentric space.

Sunderland concluded that the phenomenon of neglect in scene description was the consequence not so much of an inability to construct the left side of a visual image of a scene, as of a failure to retrieve information concerning the features on the left-hand side of an apparently intact visual image, caused by the reduced awareness of one side of the egocentric environment that characterises unilateral neglect.

Nevertheless, subsequent research indicated that "neglect" was not a unitary clinical feature but one that could be shown in several different and dissociable ways (Halligan & Marshall, 1992; Marshall et al., 1993). In particular, many patients who exhibit neglect on conventional perceptual tasks such as line cancellation do not exhibit neglect on representational tasks such as describing familiar scenes or geographical locations (see B. Anderson, 1993; Bartolomeo, D'Erme, & Gainotti, 1994). Conversely, one patient who was tested 16 months after a stroke by Guariglia, Padovani, Pantano, and Pizzamiglio (1993) showed left-sided neglect when he tried to describe urban scenes with which he was familiar or a room which he had just seen for the first time, but not when he was asked to carry out other tests that involved perception, movement, or the generation and the manipulation of novel mental images.

The theoretical interpretation of cases of visual neglect is complicated by the fact that it is often a transient symptom which is most apparent during the first few weeks following the onset of brain damage or disease (Friedland & Weinstein, 1977). It may in addition be the object of attempts at rehabilitation, although these usually meet with mixed success and often do not transfer to patients' everyday activities (Robertson, Halligan, & Marshall, 1993). Out of a total of 60 brain-damaged patients, Bartolomeo et al. (1994) found none who demonstrated neglect on representational tasks but not on perceptual tasks, though one who had initially shown neglect on both kinds of task exhibited no perceptual neglect when retested after a period of 8 months. Bartolomeo et al. suggested that the latter patient had learned to compensate for his perceptual deficits, and that this might well have been true of the patient reported by Guariglia et al.

Nonetheless, Beschin et al. (1997) described a patient who exhibited neglect in representational tasks but who had shown no neglect in perceptual tasks at any time following his brain damage due to a stroke. Although he was not formally tested in the first 2 months following his stroke, the subsequent reports given by his wife and by his medical and nursing staff made no suggestion of any perceptual impairment in his daily behaviour. Beschin et al. inferred that representational neglect could be dissociated from perceptual neglect. More specifically, they argued that neglect in purely representational tasks resulted from a selective impairment in the activation in visuo-spatial working memory of previously acquired information.

Image and Brain

During the 1980s Kosslyn became interested in trying to express his original model of imagery as a theory concerning the brain mechanisms that were involved, and also in trying to make more explicit the links between visual imagery and visual perception (see, for example, Kosslyn, 1987). With the development of more sophisticated brain-mapping techniques, these goals became much more amenable. Accordingly, Kosslyn and Koenig (1992, Chapter 4) put forward an amended account, and in 1994 Kosslyn explained the revised model in more detail in his book, *Image and Brain*. The change in title between his earlier book and this new text reflected a fundamental difference in the resources that were available for developing and testing psychological theories.

In this book, Kosslyn adopted a quite different strategy, in devoting the first (and larger) half of the text to a very detailed theoretical account of high-level perception. He focused upon how the visual system solved five different problems in trying to identify physical objects: how to recognise objects in different locations; how to recognise objects with varying shapes; how to recognise objects under impoverished viewing conditions; how to recognise specific exemplars of a general category; and how to recognise objects embedded in visual scenes. He adopted a "protomodel" with seven basic components to address these five problems (see Figure 3.10):

- a visual buffer which held spatially organised patterns of activation and was embodied in the occipital lobe;

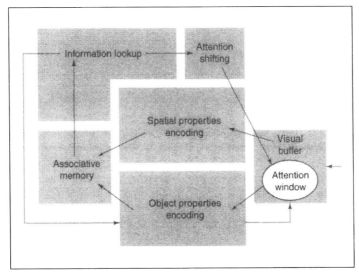

FIG. 3.10.
The "protomodel" of visual perception devised by Kosslyn (1994). From *Image and Brain: The Resolution of the Imagery Debate* (p. 69), by S.M. Kosslyn, 1994, Cambridge, MA: MIT Press. Copyright © 1994 by the MIT Press. Reprinted with permission.

- an attention window which constituted the information in the visual buffer that had been selected for further processing;
- an object properties encoding system which analysed the physical properties of objects and was embodied in the "what" or ventral system that had been identified by Ungerleider and Mishkin (1982);
- a spatial properties encoding system which analysed the spatial location and size of objects and was embodied in the "where" or dorsal system that had been identified by Ungerleider and Mishkin (1982);
- an associative memory containing information about the physical and conceptual properties of objects, which could be accessed by inputs from the ventral and dorsal encoding systems and appeared to be embodied in the posterior superior temporal lobes;
- an information-lookup device which used stored information to guide further encoding in order to collect further information about an object in a "top-down" mode when the input did not initially implicate a specific object and which appeared to be embodied in the dorsolateral prefrontal cortex;
- a system which shifted the focus of attention to different locations (either by actually shifting the body, head, eyes, or attention window or by priming the representation of a feature being sought) and which depended upon mechanisms in the frontal lobes, the posterior parietal lobes, the pulvinar, and the superior colliculus (see Kosslyn, 1994, pp. 70–74).

Kosslyn went on to elaborate this protomodel into a more closely specified account of visual perception containing no fewer than 15 components or subsystems. The model is fairly similar to that contained in his 1980 book, but there are three major differences. First, the later model was motivated in the first instance purely by the study of perceptual phenomena, without any reference to research findings concerning visual imagery. Second, he nevertheless argued that the mechanisms responsible for the generation of visual images constitute an essential part of the processes that underlie normal object recognition and are not simply parasitic upon perception. It follows that any adequate account of high-level visual perception will itself provide the foundations for a theory of visual imagery. Third, on the basis of the large amount of neuropsychological research that had been carried out in the meantime, Kosslyn was able to make specific proposals with regard to the neuroanatomical localisation of each of the postulated subsystems (as I indicated in the summary above).

In the second half of the book, Kosslyn argued that essentially the same model can account for a wide range of research findings concerning visual imagery. In the context of this model, a visual mental image is a pattern of activation in the visual buffer that has not been caused by immediate sensory input (p. 74). Kosslyn examined the production, maintenance, interpretation, and transformation of visual images, and he showed that his model could account for these processes with the addition of one further subsystem which was also claimed to play a role in visual perception. In the broadest terms, the model was not very different from its predecessor, but it was grounded in a very detailed account of visual perception and a wealth of new neuropsychological data. In its details, this model, too, may well turn out to be in need of revision. For instance, Kosslyn claimed that the visual buffer corresponded to areas within the primary visual cortex which maintained the mapping of the retina (p. 99), but (as I pointed out both above and in Chapter 2) the most recent evidence indicates that the primary visual cortex is not involved in either the function of visual imagery (M.S. Cohen et al., 1996) or the experience of visual imagery (D'Esposito et al., 1997; Mellet et al., 1995). Nevertheless, Kosslyn did succeed in providing a single integrated account of high-level visual perception and visual mental imagery.

Summary: Imagery as an internal representation

1. Imagery plays an important role in tests of spatial ability. Performance is unrelated to the vividness of imagery in general but is related to the quality of imagery experienced while carrying out the task.
2. Imagined objects can be compared along both physical and abstract dimensions and can be manipulated in a manner that is analogous to the way in which physical objects can be compared and manipulated.
3. Both the use and the phenomenal experience of visual imagery depend upon a system of visuo-spatial working memory that contains a visual buffer in which images can be constructed on the basis of information about the appearance of physical objects held in long-term memory.

4. The study of split-brain patients has indicated that the mechanisms responsible for generating coherent mental images are located within the left hemisphere, although the right hemisphere may well play a major role in the transformation of mental images.
5. Unilateral neglect usually arises in perceptual tasks, but it can also occur in representational tasks where it seems to result from a selective impairment in the activation of information stored within visuo-spatial working memory.
6. A limited amount of evidence from patients with organic disorders and from physiological recording suggests that the left inferior occipital region is implicated in image generation, but not the primary visual cortex.

Imagery as a stimulus attribute 4

In Chapter 2, I discussed the arousal of mental imagery as a phenomenal or subjective experience. I focused on differences between different people in the extent to which they tend to experience vivid and controllable images, but it is equally possible to consider differences between different materials in the extent to which they evoke vivid and controllable images. In other words, imagery can be investigated as an attribute or property of the materials or the "stimuli" that are presented to the participants in the course of psychological research.

In Chapter 3, I discussed the role of mental imagery as a kind of internal representation in which information about the visual appearance of objects could be depicted and manipulated within a visual buffer or working memory. Here, too, I focused on differences between different people in the extent to which they were able to make use of such representations when they were carrying out tests of spatial ability, but it is equally possible to consider differences between different materials in the extent to which they can be represented in such a fashion.

Indeed, I described research which had compared people's ability to deal with information about the appearance of physical objects and their ability to deal with more abstract kinds of information. It would be reasonable to assume that the former would be helped by the use of imagery, whereas the latter would not. More generally, however, this once again illustrates the important point that materials or stimuli which people encounter in psychological research vary in the ease and the speed with which they evoke imagery. This is the topic of the present chapter.

Imageability

If they so choose, researchers are at perfect liberty to define the ease with which different materials evoke mental imagery on a purely personal or intuitive basis. For instance, probably everyone would agree that the words *apple* and *elephant* tend to arouse mental images relatively quickly and easily, whereas the words *fact* and *thing* do so with difficulty or else not at all. Nevertheless, if researchers want to ensure that their personal definition has any generality and that their own intuitions are similar to those of other people (and in particular to those of their experimental subjects), they need to obtain evidence to validate their selection of experimental material. In imagery research, this is usually carried out with the assistance of questionnaires given to large groups of subjects, in which the ease with which items evoke imagery is scored along some scale.

The first large-scale study of this nature was carried out by Paivio, Yuille, and Madigan (1968), who asked 30 subjects to rate 925 nouns along a 7-point scale whose ends were labelled "Low Imagery" (rating 1) and "High Imagery" (rating 7). The instructions used by Paivio et al. are shown in Box 4.1. A measure of the imagery value or *imageability* of each item was obtained by taking the average rating across all the subjects. Those items which are given relatively high average ratings on this scale are often described as "high-imagery" items, whereas those items which are given relatively low average ratings are described as "low-imagery" items. Research carried out during the 1960s and 1970s showed that high-imagery items tended to be remembered better than low-imagery items across a wide variety of learning tasks (see Paivio, 1971, Chapter 7).

In Chapter 2, I pointed out that people show a great deal of variability in reports of the vividness of their experienced imagery, and one might therefore expect concomitant variability in their ratings of the imageability of individual words. This idea has not received very much attention, but two studies have reported gender

Box 4.1.
Imageability rating
instructions.
From
"Concreteness,
imagery, and
meaningfulness
values for 925
nouns", by A.
Paivio, J.C. Yuille,
and S.A. Madigan,
1968, *Journal of
Experimental
Psychology
Monographs, 76*
(1, Pt. 2), 4.
Copyright © 1968
by the American
Psychological
Association, Inc.
Reprinted with
permission.

Nouns differ in their capacity to arouse mental images of things or events. Some words arouse a sensory experience, such as a mental picture or sound, very quickly and easily, whereas others may do so only with difficulty (i.e., after a long delay) or not at all. The purpose of this experiment is to rate a list of words as to the ease or difficulty with which they arouse mental images. Any word which, in your estimation, arouses a mental image (i.e., a mental picture, or sound, or other sensory experience) very quickly and easily should be given a *high imagery* rating; any word that arouses a mental image with difficulty or not at all should be given a *low imagery* rating. Think of the words "apple" and "fact". Apple would probably arouse an image relatively easily and would be rated as high imagery; fact would probably do so with difficulty and would be rated as low imagery. Since words tend to make you think of other words as associates, e.g., knife–fork, it is important that you note only the ease of getting a mental image of an object or an event to the word.

differences in the distribution of imageability ratings. Friendly, Franklin, Hoffman, and Rubin (1982) obtained responses from 200 students for 1080 common English words, and they found no difference between the mean ratings given by men and women. However, Benjafield and Muckenheim (1989) collected responses from 30 students on 1046 words chosen at random from the entire *Oxford English Dictionary,* and they found that women gave significantly higher ratings than men overall.

The size of the gender difference obtained by Benjafield and Muckenheim was fairly small (0.20 of a scale point), but, taken together, these results might suggest that women tend to give higher ratings to rare words than men. This difference is apparently specific to imageability ratings, since Benjafield and Muckenheim found that men gave higher ratings than women when rating the same words on their concreteness (see below). This is consistent with the finding that women tend to report more vivid imagery than men, as was pointed out in Chapter 2. Nevertheless, the gender difference obtained by Benjafield and Muckenheim could simply have arisen from the use of small and possibly unrepresentative samples of male and female subjects.

Although they found no difference in the mean imageability ratings given by men and women, Friendly et al. (1982) did find a greater level of dispersion in women's ratings than in men's: in other words, women appeared to make somewhat more use of the extreme points on the rating scale. This effect was apparently not specific to imageability ratings: Friendly et al. found the same result in 200 other students who gave concreteness ratings on the same words, and they noted that Toglia and Battig (1978, p. 7) had found a similar pattern for ratings of pleasantness. Thus, women tend to produce a broader distribution of ratings than men across a variety of semantic properties. Given that the objects and scenes that have to be rated in questionnaires on the vividness of experienced imagery are highly imageable, this result is consistent with the view that gender differences in the scores obtained on these questionnaires are due just to women's use of more lenient decision criteria (see Chapter 2).

In both of these studies, the authors identified words for which the mean ratings produced by men and women differed by at least 0.5. These represented a higher proportion of the samples of words than would have been expected just by chance: 414/1080 for the study by Friendly et al. and 484/1046 for the study by Benjafield and Muckenheim. No attempt was made in either study to categorise the kinds of words that generated differences in one direction or the other, although the fact that women show a greater level of dispersion than men in their responses implies that women would give higher ratings to high-imagery words and lower ratings to low-imagery words. Nevertheless, the authors of both these studies stressed that in general the mean ratings given by men and women correlated very highly with each other.

Moreover, it is doubtful whether individual differences in imageability ratings have implications for objective cognitive performance. I conducted two experiments in which the subjects rated the imageability of either words or pairs of words and were then unexpectedly asked to recall the items that they had rated (J.T.E. Richardson, 1979a). The correlation coefficient between the mean imagery rating given by each subject and the number of items recalled by that subject was -0.07 in the first experiment and $+0.12$ in the second experiment, neither of which was at all significant. In short, imageability ratings predict variations in performance across different items but not across different subjects. On reflection, this is perhaps not at all surprising, given that the instructions fix the end-points of the rating scale in terms of each respondent's experience of imagery (see Box 4.1). Although subjects may vary in how they distribute their ratings across the entire scale, the range of responses is essentially determined in advance and is unlikely to have predictive value.

It will be noted that the instructions used by Paivio et al. (1968) emphasised the ease with which mental imagery was evoked by a word. In principle, one could instead obtain ratings of the vividness of the evoked imagery, which would be more in keeping with the questionnaires that were discussed in Chapter 2. Some researchers have in fact obtained vividness ratings, but these tend to be highly correlated with the ease of image arousal and do not in themselves appear to be very important in determining performance in memory tasks (see J.T.E. Richardson, 1980b, pp. 85–86).

This was demonstrated in an experiment by Neisser and Kerr (1973), who asked their subjects to rate the vividness of the imagery that was evoked by three different kinds of sentence. Some sentences described pairs of objects in a way that would encourage mental images in which the two objects were depicted as separated in imaginal space (i.e. "separative" imagery):

> Looking from one window, you see the Statue of Liberty;
> from a window in another wall, you see a daffodil.

Other sentences described pairs of objects in an interacting, picturable relationship (i.e. "pictorial" interactive imagery):

A daffodil is sitting on top of the torch held up by the Statue of Liberty.

Finally, other sentences described pairs of objects in an interacting relationship, but not one that could be represented by an ordinary two-dimensional picture ("concealed" interactive imagery):

A daffodil is hidden inside the torch held up by the Statue of Liberty.

Neisser and Kerr found that the "pictorial" images were rated as more vivid than the "separative" or "concealed" images, which were given similar vividness ratings. However, when the subjects were unexpectedly asked to recall the sentences after carrying out the rating task, the "concealed" sentences were recalled as well as the "pictorial" sentences and better than the "separative" sentences. This confirms the general observation which I made in Chapter 3, that the functional value of mental imagery is largely unrelated to its vividness.

To explain the effectiveness of imageability in predicting memory performance, Paivio (1971) proposed that there were two different systems of coding or representation that people could use: images and verbal processes. Subsequently, Paivio (1978d) spelled out this "dual coding theory" in the following manner (see Figure 4.1):

The theory assumes that cognitive behavior is mediated by two independent but richly interconnected symbolic systems that are specialized for encoding, organizing, transforming, storing, and retrieving information. One (the image system) is specialized for dealing with perceptual information concerning nonverbal objects and events. The other (the verbal system) is specialized for dealing with linguistic information. The systems differ in the nature of the representational units, the way the units are organized into higher-order structures, and the way the structures can be reorganized or transformed. (p. 379)

Paivio (1975a) suggested that their intrinsic functions "distinguish the verbal system as an abstract, logical mode of thinking, as compared to the concrete, analogical mode that apparently characterizes imagery" (p. 148). This relates to the assumption that the two systems were different in the way that their units were organised into higher-order structures. The image system was assumed to represent information in a "synchronous" or spatially parallel

FIG. 4.1. A simplified schematisation of the dual-coding model. From "The relationship between verbal and perceptual codes", by A. Paivio, 1978, in E.C. Carterette and M.P. Friedman (Ed.), *Handbook of Perception: Vol. VIII. Perceptual Coding*, p. 381, New York: Academic Press. Copyright © 1978 by Academic Press, Inc. Reprinted with permission.

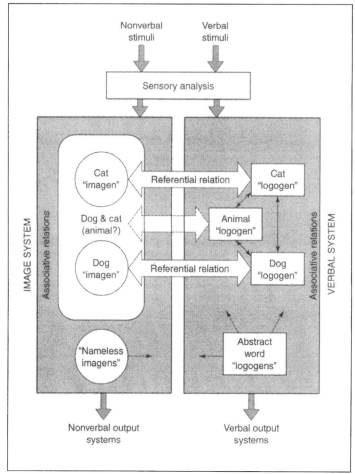

manner, so that different components of a complex object or scene were simultaneously available; however, the verbal system was taken to employ the sequential organisation which is characteristic of linguistic utterances. Similarly, the image system was assumed to be capable of transformations along spatial dimensions, such as size, shape, and orientation, whereas the verbal system was taken to allow transformations on a sequential basis, such as additions, deletions, and changes in sequential ordering (see also Paivio, 1986).

Within this model, Paivio (1971, p. 53; 1978d) identified three levels at which information might be processed. The first was the *representational* level, where the sensory trace that was produced by an item when it was perceived arouses the appropriate symbolic representation in long-term memory. Thus, words activated verbal representations (which Paivio called "logogens"), whereas perceptual experiences activated imaginal representations (which he called "imagens"). The second was the *referential* level, where symbolic representations in one system aroused corresponding representations in the other system; these interconnections were assumed to be involved in naming or describing objects, on the one hand, and in creating the image of an object when given its name, on the other hand. Finally, the *associative* level involved associative connections among images, among verbal representations, or among both.

Whether the processes at any of these three levels were involved in a given psychological task depended upon particular characteristics of the task, but in learning and remembering all three levels were assumed potentially to be implicated. Consequently, performance could be based upon the image system, the verbal system, or both. This was then linked to another assumption, the "coding redundancy hypothesis". This stated that memory performance increased directly with the number of alternative memory codes available for an item (Paivio, 1971, p. 181). Given these assumptions, the fact that retention increases with the imageability of the material can be explained

> because the items are increasingly likely to be stored in *both* the verbal and the nonverbal code. . . . The increased availability of both codes increases the probability of item recall because the response can be retrieved from either code—one code could be forgotten during the retention interval, but verbal recall would still be possible provided that the other is retained. (Paivio, 1971, pp. 207–208)

Concreteness

Nevertheless, the difference between words such as *apple* and *elephant* and words such as *fact* and *thing* can be characterised in other ways that have nothing to do with the image-arousing potential of the material. A quite natural way of describing these two sets of nouns would be to say that the former were relatively *concrete* while the latter were relatively *abstract*, in the sense that they cannot be directly experienced through the senses.

Paivio et al. (1968) acknowledged the existence of a separate dimension of concreteness, and they asked 28 subjects to rate the same set of 925 nouns on a 7-point scale whose ends were labelled "highly abstract" (1) and "highly concrete" (7). The instructions explained:

> Any word that refers to objects, materials, or persons should receive a *high concreteness* rating; any word that refers to an abstract concept that cannot be experienced by the senses should receive a *high abstractness* rating. (p. 5)

Once again, a measure of the concreteness of each item was obtained by taking the average score across all the subjects. Although the two sets of ratings had been collected from two different groups, the mean imageability and concreteness scores were very highly correlated across the 925 words, and Paivio (1971, p. 79) inferred that concreteness and imageability were essentially measuring the same underlying variable.

In some other fields, such as linguistics, developmental psychology, or philosophy, the distinction between concrete and abstract words is often taken to be a fundamental property of the way in which language is organised (J.T.E. Richardson, 1980c). There is some empirical evidence for this kind of interpretation in experiments on semantic memory, which tend to show effects of concreteness but not of imageability when the two variables are varied independently (J.T.E. Richardson, 1975a, 1980a). This means that one should not regard concreteness just as an alternative measure of imageability. Nevertheless, the application of multiple regression analysis to data from memory experiments shows that it is the imageability of the material rather than its concreteness which is the effective attribute determining how easily it can be remembered (J.T.E. Richardson, 1980c). In other words, memory for high-imagery items is more efficient than memory for low-imagery items, but this is not simply because high-imagery items refer to concrete objects, materials, and persons and hence are more likely to involve perceptual or spatial information.

A number of other properties have been suggested to try to explain the superior memorability of high-imagery material in purely linguistic terms. For instance, Kintsch (1972) proposed that concrete nouns were grammatically simple and basic whereas abstract nouns were somehow derived from concrete nouns and hence were grammatically complex. J.R. Anderson and Bower (1973, p. 458) argued that concrete words had fewer different dictionary meanings and more semantic features than abstract words. G.V. Jones (1988) suggested that there were more potential properties (or "predicates") that could be attached to concrete words than to abstract words. On accounts of this sort, concrete items should be *inherently* more memorable than abstract words unless there were some catastrophic disruption of the individual's command of language. Conversely, if the effect of imageability is attributable to a specific process or strategy based upon the use of imagery, then it should be possible to disrupt this process or strategy and to eliminate the effect by appropriate procedures or as the result of certain forms of brain damage.

Paivio (1972) pointed out that increasing the rate at which different items were presented was one way of selectively interfering with cognitive processing. Concrete or abstract words can be named faster than they can be imaged, and hence one would expect that access to imaginal encoding would be disrupted by use of a fast rate of presentation. In contrast, if the effect of imageability is simply a consequence of how concrete and abstract words are represented within a common semantic system, the effect should be largely independent of presentation rate. In fact, there is some evidence that the effect is reduced with very fast rates of presentation, which Paivio took as support for his dual coding theory.

In Chapter 3, I described various experiments showing that visual short-term memory could be disrupted by making people carry out concurrent spatial tasks (such as tracking a moving target) or by presenting irrelevant visual stimuli (such as patterns or coloured patches). If the effect of imageability is based upon some process involving imagery, then one might expect these procedures to interfere with that process and so reduce the effect of imageability. In fact, several studies have found that concurrent visuo-motor tasks may reduce the overall level of performance in remembering lists of words, but they do not significantly reduce the effect of imageability (Baddeley, Grant, Wight, & Thomson, 1975; Byrne, 1974; Warren, 1977). However, other researchers have found that presenting irrelevant visual stimuli does produce a significant reduction in the effect of imageability (Janssen, 1976a, 1976b; Matthews, 1983). This suggests that the effect is based upon a process involving the visual buffer (Kosslyn, 1980, 1994) or passive visual store (Logie, 1995), but not upon the form of spatial rehearsal that is responsible for refreshing that store.

Imageability and hemispheric asymmetries

In Chapter 1, I mentioned the well-established finding of a functional dissociation between the two cerebral hemispheres with respect to the processing of verbal and non-verbal information. Paivio (1971, pp. 522–523; 1978b) regarded this as direct support for his dual coding theory of imagery and verbal symbolic functioning (see also Sheikh, 1977). Is it possible, therefore, to relate the effects of imageability to the phenomenon of the cerebral lateralisation of function?

As I also mentioned in Chapter 1, the recognition of individual words tends to be better when they are displayed in the right visual hemifield than when they are displayed in the left visual hemifield. This is in accord with the notion that in most normal subjects the left hemisphere has the primary responsibility for language processing. During the 1970s, a number of researchers found that this right visual-field superiority was attenuated or even abolished in the case of concrete, imageable material. This finding suggested the hypothesis that "the right cerebral hemisphere in normal subjects may possess a selective ability to understand highly imageable words" (Lambert & Beaumont, 1981, p. 411). This is consistent with the fact that certain patients with lesions in the left hemisphere show a selective impairment in the reading of abstract words (Coltheart, 1980): on this interpretation, these patients can use the residual capacity of their intact right hemisphere to read at least some concrete words.

Nevertheless, as Ehrlichman and Barrett (1983) pointed out, the claim is simply that the right hemisphere is better able to recognise high-imagery words than low-imagery words, and not that the (intact) right hemisphere is better able to recognise high-imagery words than the left hemisphere (an idea for which there is no evidence whatsoever). It is also unclear whether it is the image-arousing quality of verbal material or its concreteness that determines the degree of asymmetry in the recognition of words displayed in the left and right hemifields (Bruyer & Racquez, 1985). In fact, Young (1987) noted that only around half of all published experiments had found a difference in the magnitude of the right visual-field superiority obtained between concrete and abstract words, and he inferred that these sporadic effects were likely to be due to a confounded variable or a procedural artefact. In short, this kind of experiment can contribute little to debates over whether imagery is implicated in reading or whether imagery is a right-hemisphere function.

Haynes and Moore (1981) made electroencephalographic recordings from sites in the temporal and parietal lobes whilst their subjects were learning sentences which were composed of either high-imagery words or low-imagery words. The efficacy of this manipulation was shown by the fact that the subjects' subsequent recall of the high-imagery sentences was greatly superior to that of the low-imagery sentences. Nevertheless, there was no sign of any difference between the two conditions in terms of the relative levels of alpha suppression (implying brain activation) in the two cerebral hemispheres. This would suggest that imageability taps mechanisms in both hemispheres.

Goldenberg, Podreka, Steiner, and Willmes (1987) carried out a similar experiment in which cerebral blood flow across 30 different regions was measured whilst the subjects attempted to learn lists of 12 high-imagery nouns or 12 low-imagery nouns. The overall level of activation showed a slight rightward shift when they were learning the concrete nouns, but this effect was not statistically significant. Indeed, there was no significant difference between the two conditions across any of the regions studied. However, in this experiment the data are difficult to evaluate, because the lists of high-imagery and low-imagery words produced identical levels of performance in a subsequent retention test; consequently, there was no internal evidence in this study that the subjects had been using mental imagery in order to learn the high-imagery material at all.

Some researchers have examined the effects of imageability in patients with brain lesions confined to just one cerebral hemisphere. For instance, M.K. Jones (1974) tested 36 patients who had undergone surgical resection of one or other of the temporal lobes for the relief of chronic epilepsy. Previous research had shown that patients with lesions of the left temporal lobe were impaired in verbal learning and memory, but not in the retention of complex visual displays which could not be readily described or labelled; conversely, patients with lesions of the right temporal lobe were impaired on non-verbal memory tasks, but not in verbal memory tasks (Milner, 1966, 1971). Jones asked her subjects to learn a single list of 10 high-imagery and low-imagery paired associates over three trials. In terms of their overall performance, the patients with lesions of the left temporal lobe showed a significant impairment compared with a normal control group, whereas those with lesions of the right temporal lobe did not. However, both groups of patients demonstrated the normal pattern of superior recall of high-imagery words compared with low-imagery words.

The same pattern of results in patients with unilateral temporal lobectomy was obtained by Jones-Gotman (1979) using an incidental learning paradigm and by Petrides and Milner (1982) using a task in which the subjects monitored their sequences of responses to arrays of high-imagery and low-imagery words. Shore (1979) carried out a similar investigation in which 48 patients with circumscribed brain damage were tested on their recall of a list that contained six high-imagery words and six low-imagery words. Once again, the patients with damage to the left hemisphere were significantly impaired relative to a group of 24 normal control subjects, but those patients with damage to the right hemisphere were not impaired. All three groups showed equivalent effects of imageability on their recall.

Subsequently, Goldenberg (1989) compared the performance of 74 patients with unilateral brain damage due to a variety of causes with that of 59 control patients with peripheral lesions on the recall of paired associates. The patients with damage confined to the right hemisphere were unimpaired on both high-imagery words and low-imagery words and showed a normal effect of imageability. The patients with damage confined to the left hemisphere were profoundly impaired on both sorts of material, and they showed no significant effect of imageability in their performance. The latter outcome could be taken to reflect a specific inability to enhance verbal memory by using imagery, but Goldenberg himself ascribed the results to a floor effect: in other words, the patients were already performing so poorly on the high-imagery words that there was little scope for them to perform any worse on the low-imagery words.

In short, patients who have brain lesions confined to just one cerebral hemisphere—and in particular those patients who have lesions confined to the right cerebral hemisphere—tend to show effects of imageability in learning and remembering that are generally equivalent in magnitude to those which are shown by normal control subjects. It is therefore not possible to ascribe such effects to neural mechanisms within either of the cerebral hemispheres.

Imageability effects and brain dysfunction

Most patients who have suffered more generalised brain damage also seem to demonstrate the normal pattern of better retention of high-imagery words than on low-imagery words. This has been found in patients with brain lesions that are circumscribed but encroach upon both hemispheres (Goldenberg, 1989), patients who have undergone microsurgical treatment following the rupture of an intracranial aneurysm (J.T.E. Richardson, 1989), and patients with Parkinson's disease (Goldenberg, 1989). In themselves, these findings are of little theoretical interest, except insofar as they show that the results of laboratory experiments which have been carried out with groups of college students do generalise to a broader population. However, two groups of patients with diffuse cerebral damage have been identified who, under certain circumstances, at least, do not show effects of imageability on their memory performance.

The first group consists of patients who have received a "closed" head injury. This is an injury to the head in which the primary mechanism of damage is one of blunt impact. Such injuries are common in all industrialised countries (mainly as the result of road traffic accidents, domestic falls, assaults, occupational injuries, and recreational accidents), and they characteristically give rise to impaired performance on tests of learning and remembering (J.T.E. Richardson, 1990). I carried out a study to compare 40 patients with minor closed head injuries with a control group of 40 orthopaedic patients (J.T.E. Richardson, 1979b). All the patients were tested on their immediate recall of each of five lists of high-imagery words and five lists of low-imagery words, and they then received an unexpected final recall test on all the words presented. The results are shown in Table 4.1.

The head-injured patients were found to be impaired in the recall of lists of high-imagery words but not in the recall of lists of low-imagery words. The control patients demonstrated the usual pattern of better recall of high-imagery words than of low-imagery words. Nevertheless, the head-injured patients showed no significant advantage in their recall of high-imagery material. This pattern was

TABLE 4.1

	Initial testing		Final testing	
	Concrete	Abstract	Concrete	Abstract
Orthopaedic controls	46.9	35.3	17.4	10.8
Head-injured patients	41.6	36.7	12.2	10.5

Mean per cent correct in free recall for head-injured patients and for orthopaedic control subjects on concrete and abstract material in initial and final testing. From "Mental imagery, human memory, and the effects of closed head injury", by J.T.E. Richardson, 1979, *British Journal of Social and Clinical Psychology*, *18*, 322. Copyright © 1979 by the British Psychological Society. Reprinted with permission.

obtained both on the immediate test and on the final, cumulative test. I proposed that closed head injuries gave rise to a specific problem in the use of imagery as a form of elaborative encoding in long-term memory. One of my students and I found essentially the same results in a later study that included both severe and minor cases of closed head injury (J.T.E. Richardson & Snape, 1984).

I also obtained further evidence in support of my proposal by analysing the intrusion errors from previous lists which had been produced by the patients in my original study (J.T.E. Richardson, 1984). The findings are summarised in Table 4.2. The control patients showed a strong tendency to produce intrusion errors that were of similar imageability to the list they were trying to remember: in other words, most intrusion errors produced in trying to recall high-imagery lists came from previous high-imagery lists, and most intrusion errors produced in trying to recall low-imagery lists came from previous low-imagery lists. Nevertheless, the head-injured patients showed no sign of this effect: the imageability of their intrusion errors was totally unrelated to the imageability of the list that they were trying to recall. This appeared to confirm the idea that closed head injuries impaired retention by disrupting the patients' normal encoding of the image-evoking quality of the material.

The second group of patients in whom results of this sort have been found consists of people with Huntington's disease. This is a form of degenerative dementia that tends to involve a progressive impairment of memory function (see Kapur, 1988, pp. 126–128, 140). Weingartner, Caine, and Ebert (1979a, 1979b) compared eight

TABLE 4.2

	Concrete lists	Abstract lists	Total
Control patients			
Concrete intrusions	58	28	86
Abstract intrusions	20	58	78
Total	78	86	164
Head-injured patients			
Concrete intrusions	37	31	68
Abstract intrusions	46	45	91
Total	83	76	159

Numbers of prior-list intrusion errors given by head-injured patients and orthopaedic control subjects in the immediate free recall of concrete and abstract lists of words. From "The effects of closed head injury upon intrusions and confusions in free recall", by J.T.E. Richardson, 1984, *Cortex*, *20*, 416. Copyright © 1984 by Masson Italia Periodici S.r.l. Reprinted with permission.

patients with Huntington's disease with eight normal control subjects on their recall of a list that contained 10 high-imagery words and 10 low-imagery words. They used a "selective reminding" procedure which was developed by Buschke (1973). In this procedure, subjects are tested over several trials, but only the items that are *not* recalled on a given trial are presented again for learning on the subsequent trial.

Weingartner et al. found that the Huntington's patients recalled far fewer items in total and were much less consistent in their recall from one trial to the next. Moreover, whereas the control patients remembered more high-imagery words than low-imagery words, the Huntington's patients showed no sign of any difference in their recall between the two types of word. Weingartner et al. asked some of their Huntington's patients to rate the imageability of individual words, and they found that they reproduced the mean ratings that were generated by large normal samples. They concluded that Huntington's patients were sensitive to the varying imageability of words, but that they had failed to use this in encoding the items for later recall.

Most of the research evidence concerning imagery and the brain that I have described in this book comes either from the study of brain activation in normal people or from the study of the effects of brain damage in clinical patients. However, it is also possible to study brain function and brain dysfunction using psychoactive drugs. The resulting changes in cognitive function are normally reversible, and so subjects can be used as their own controls. Research of this sort is not without its methodological problems, but it provides a major source of additional evidence on the neurobiology of human learning and memory (see Lister & Weingartner, 1987; Wolkowitz, Tinklenberg, & Weingartner, 1985a). It seems that some drugs affect memory so as to remove the effect of imageability upon performance.

Many drugs are known to affect memory function by influencing the metabolism of one or more neurotransmitters. These are the chemical substances that are released by a nerve cell in order to influence or communicate with other nerve cells. The first chemical substance to be identified as a neurotransmitter was acetylcholine. This is synthesised in nerve terminals out of the organic compound choline by the action of an enzyme called choline acetyltransferase, and it is inactivated by the action of another enzyme called acetylcholinesterase (see Figure 4.2). It has been well established for many years that this system of neurochemical transmission, which is known as the cholinergic system, is involved in human learning and memory.

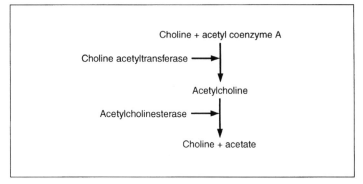

The main evidence comes from the administration of drugs to disrupt this system, and this can be achieved in a variety of ways. For instance, cholinergic antagonists such as hyoscine (which is known in the United States as "scopolamine") block the effects of acetylcholine at some receptors within the nervous system. These drugs may have a variety of behavioural effects (for instance, hyoscine is widely used as a sedative agent), but their most prominent effect from a purely cognitive point of view is to disrupt the storage of new information into long-term memory; both the retrieval of old information that was acquired before the drug's administration and the retention of recent information held in short-term memory are typically unimpaired (see Drachman & Sahakian, 1979; Kopelman, 1986).

As well as testing Huntington's patients, Weingartner et al. (1979a) studied the effects of intravenous hyoscine on the recall of high-imagery and low-imagery words in seven normal volunteers, once again using the selective reminding procedure. The drug led to poorer recall and less intertrial consistency, and it apparently also abolished the difference between high-imagery and low-imagery words. Weingartner et al. commented: "The volunteers did not utilize high imagery while learning the words as a means of encoding the test items more effectively" (p. 222). Because of the similarity between these results and those which they had obtained with their Huntington's patients, Weingartner et al. were led to raise the question whether the memory impairment in Huntington's disease was caused by some disorder of cholinergic neurotransmission.

In contrast, cholinergic *agonists* are substances that will stimulate the responses of acetylcholine receptors. This, too, can be achieved in a number of ways: by administering choline; by stimulating the release of acetylcholine; or by prolonging the action of acetylcholine by inhibiting acetylcholinesterase. Cholinergic agonists undoubtedly reverse the amnesic effects of cholinergic antagonists. If they are administered in isolation to normal volunteers, they may enhance some aspects of learning and memory in some subjects, but any effects are very slight in magnitude, unreliable, and dependent on the precise dosage (see McGeer, 1984; Wolkowitz, Tinklenberg, & Weingartner, 1985b).

Sitaram, Weingartner, Caine, and Gillin (1978) and Sitaram, Weingartner, and Gillin (1979) studied the effects of choline upon memory function. Ten normal volunteers were tested on lists containing six high-imagery words and six low-imagery words after a single oral dose of choline and also after the administration of an inactive placebo, once again using the selective reminding procedure. The administration of choline produced a selective increase in the recall of low-imagery words, to the extent that there was no longer any significant difference between the recall of high-imagery and low-imagery words. This was associated with a concomitant increase in the intertrial consistency in the recall of low-imagery words.

Unfortunately, similar findings were not obtained in an experiment that was carried out by Weingartner et al. (1979a) to evaluate the effects of the intramuscular administration of physostigmine, which is an inhibitor of acetylcholinesterase. They employed the same task as Sitaram et al., but they failed to find any statistically significant changes in performance following the administration of physostigmine. This simply illustrates the point which I made earlier that the apparently beneficial effects of cholinergic enhancers upon learning and memory are often very hard to replicate.

Nonetheless, it would appear that there are at least three circumstances in which experimental subjects do not demonstrate significant effects of imageability upon their performance in tests of learning and memory:

- patients with closed head injury tested by a conventional recall procedure;
- patients with Huntington's disease tested by the selective reminding procedure; and
- normal volunteers tested by the selective reminding procedure following the administration of hyoscine.

These findings seem to bear directly upon the plausibility of various accounts of the effects of imageability in memory that refer to linguistic properties of the items to be remembered, such as their number of dictionary meanings or their number of semantic features or predicates.

On accounts such as these, high-imagery items should be inherently more memorable than low-imagery items, regardless of the overall level of memory performance, unless there were some catastrophic disruption of the patients' understanding of word meanings. Since closed head injuries, Huntington's disease, or intravenous hyoscine do not give rise to any global problems of semantic interpretation and analysis, it is hard to explain in purely psycholinguistic terms why the effects of imageability should be abolished under these circumstances. It is certainly more congenial to interpret such a phenomenon in terms of some selective impairment in the use of mental imagery. Conversely, the substantial and reliable effects of imageability that are obtained in the recall performance of normal subjects should be ascribed to the employment of mental imagery as a memory code.

Although it does not detract from this conclusion, I ought to point out that, in two of these three circumstances, similar results are *not* obtained when more standard procedures are used to test the subjects. For instance, Frith, Richardson, Samuel, Crow, and McKenna (1984) examined the effects of intravenous hyoscine on the recall of lists of high-imagery and low-imagery words in normal volunteers. Although the drug did give rise to an appreciable decline in the absolute level of performance, it had no effect on the difference in recall between high-imagery and low-imagery words. Frith et al. concluded that hyoscine had no effect on the use of imagery as a form of memory coding.

Again, Beatty and Butters (1986) compared 12 Huntington's patients and 12 normal control subjects on their recall of a list containing seven high-imagery and seven low-imagery words. Both the Huntington's patients and the normal controls recalled more high-imagery words than low-imagery words, and the size of this effect did not differ between the two groups. In short, it would seem that people who suffer from memory dysfunction as the result of Huntington's disease or the administration of anticholinergic drugs are perfectly able to use mental imagery as a memory code in conventional memory tasks, but that they are led to abandon this in the selective-reminding procedure.

Dual coding or dual processing?

In Paivio's (1971) dual coding theory, the verbal system was supposed to be specialised for serial or sequential processing, whereas the image system was supposed to be specialised for simultaneous or parallel processing. It follows from this that the image system should not be important in tasks that involve the retention of a familiar set of verbal items in a particular sequence, such as immediate memory span. Instead, performance on these tasks should depend solely upon the efficiency of the verbal system. According to the coding redundancy hypothesis, observed effects of imageability reflect the involvement of the image system. Conversely, therefore, if the image system is not involved in certain tasks, performance should not vary with the imageability of the materials. Paivio noted that there was support for this, insofar as memory span for high-imagery nouns did not seem to differ from memory span for low-imagery nouns.

The source which Paivio cited for this result was a study by Brener (1940), who measured students' memory spans on a wide variety of materials. When sequences were presented visually, Brener estimated the memory span at 5.76 items for high-imagery nouns and 5.24 items for low-imagery nouns; when sequences were presented auditorily, the corresponding means were 5.86 and 5.58 items, respectively. Although there was clearly a trend for high-imagery nouns to be better remembered, Brener argued that "no clear differentiation should be made in the order of difficulty" (p. 473). Moreover, most of Brener's high-imagery nouns contained just one syllable, but most of his low-imagery nouns contained two syllables. It is now known that the length of the relevant items is a primary determinant of memory span (Baddeley, Thomson, & Buchanan, 1975), and this variable would therefore explain the small trend apparent in Brener's data.

Nevertheless, in memory tasks that involve the acquisition of specific items, and especially in tasks that do *not* involve the retention of serial order, Paivio (1971) was explicit that the image system would be used, and therefore that imageability should be directly correlated with performance (pp. 178, 234). Such tasks would include

- recognition memory, in which subjects are presented with individual items and are asked to judge whether or not they were among those that had been presented previously for learning;
- free recall, in which subjects are presented with lists of items and then attempt to recall them in any order;
- paired-associate learning, in which subjects learn pairs of items and are then tested by being cued or prompted with one of the items in each pair and have to respond with the other item in the pair.

It is true that imageability effects are normally obtained in all of these tasks. There is, however, a problem. The dual coding theory attributes imageability effects to the activation of representations in the image system (see Figure 4.1). Since it attributes such effects to intrinsic properties of the items being learned, it must predict that such effects would be found in any experimental task that involves the acquisition of high-imagery and low-imagery materials. (This observation was first made by Marschark, Richman, Yuille, and Hunt, 1987 with regard to effects of imageability in paired-associate learning.) The absence of imageability effects following brain damage or drugs could be ascribed to a selective disruption of the associative connections between the verbal and image systems, but there are a number of situations in which the effects of imageability are reduced or abolished altogether even in normal individuals.

Begg (1972) asked his subjects to remember adjective–noun phrases and compared their performance in a free-recall test with their performance when they had been cued with either the adjective or the noun. He found that cueing led to an increase in recall on high-imagery phrases (such as *square door*), but that there was no such improvement on low-imagery phrases (such as *impossible amount*). Although the high-imagery phrases were better remembered than the low-imagery phrases even under free recall, the effect was much smaller than that obtained under cued recall. Begg initially interpreted his findings in terms of the likelihood that high-imagery and low-imagery phrases would give rise to integrated images. However, he subsequently came to the conclusion that they reflected general properties of memory organisation rather than any peculiarity of mental imagery (Begg, 1978).

I carried out a similar experiment using nominalisations, which are English phrases constructed by combining participles and nouns (J.T.E. Richardson, 1975b). These can be constructed in two different ways. In subject nominalisations (e.g. *barking dogs* or *astonishing beliefs*), the noun is the logical subject of the verb (*dogs bark, beliefs astonish*). In object nominalisations (e.g. *mashing potatoes* or *adopting methods*), the noun is the logical object of the verb and the logical subject is left unspecified (*someone mashes potatoes, someone adopts methods*). Nevertheless, I found that there was no difference between how easily the two kinds of phrases could be remembered. High-imagery phrases (e.g. *barking dogs* or *mashing potatoes*) were better recalled than low-imagery phrases (e.g. *astonishing beliefs* or *adopting methods*) when the subjects were cued with either the participle or the verb in question. However, the effect of imageability was not statistically significant when the subjects were simply tested by free recall.

Earlier in this chapter, I referred to another study that involved incidental-learning experiments in which the subjects rated materials in terms of their imageability and were then unexpectedly asked to recall the materials which they had been rating (J.T.E. Richardson, 1979a). In one experiment, subjects rated pairs of words in terms of the ease with which they aroused a mental image in which the two things were interrelated or were interacting in some way. They were then provided with the first member in each pair and had to recall the word which had been presented with it. Across 30 pairs of words, the correlation coefficient between the mean imagery rating and the likelihood of correct recall was +0.67, which was very highly significant.

In a different experiment, the subjects rated individual words in terms of their imageability, as defined by Paivio et al. (1968). They were then unexpectedly asked to recall any of the words which they had rated in any order. Across 30 words, the correlation coefficient between the mean imagery rating and the likelihood of correct recall was only +0.28, which was not statistically significant. Taken together, then, these results confirm that interactive imagery is an important determinant of recall performance, but that separative imagery is not.

Marschark (1985) constructed narrative passages containing either high-imagery or low-imagery sentences. He found that high-imagery sentences were remembered better than low-imagery sentences when they were presented in a random order, but that performance was equivalent on the high-imagery and low-imagery sentences when they were presented within coherent passages. Marschark noted that these findings were not consistent with Paivio's (1971) dual coding theory. He suggested that in learning randomly ordered sentences (where the relational context was relatively weak) the use of imagery enhanced the distinctiveness of high-imagery material and thus rendered it more memorable than low-imagery material. However, when the same sentences were being learned in coherent passages, the narrative structure provided a rich relational context for both high-imagery and low-imagery materials that made the subjects' use of mental imagery unnecessary.

A key feature of Marschark's experiment was that he used a between-subjects manipulation of text imageability. Marschark, Cornoldi, Huffman, Pé, and Garzari (1994) confirmed that, when imageability is manipulated between subjects, it had no effect upon text retention. Effects of imageability can sometimes be obtained using a within-subjects design, and these are mainly associated with superior recall of high-imagery texts after the subjects have already learned low-imagery texts. These results are consistent with the view that the effects of imageability are reduced or abolished using a between-subjects manipulation because high-imagery and low-imagery texts activate relational (or macropropositional) processing (Marschark et al., 1987). However, the presentation of high-imagery materials after low-imagery materials appears to provide some additional source of distinctiveness (possibly recency), and it therefore enhances their recall relative to that of low-imagery materials.

Marschark et al. (1987) suggested that a general problem with earlier research was that it had failed to distinguish between imaginal and verbal processing, on the one hand, and between imaginal and verbal storage, on the other hand. (Some philosophers of mind would in an analogous way differentiate between imagery as a mental act or process and imagery as the product or content of that act or process.) Marschark et al. agreed that effects of imageability upon recall were evidence for the distinction between imaginal and verbal processing, but they argued that the absence of such effects under particular procedural manipulations was evidence against the distinction between imaginal and verbal storage. Instead, they argued that effects of imageability could be attributed to the enhanced distinctiveness of the items and especially to the enhanced encoding of relationships amongst them. These effects could be eliminated either by preventing subjects from using encoded relationships (for instance, by the use of free recall in the experiments by Begg and myself) or by providing an alternative basis for encoding relational information (as with thematically structured narrative materials in Marschark's experiments).

Marschark and Hunt (1989) tested this account with a range of experiments using conventional paired-associate learning, in which the subjects were cued with one of the words in each pair and had to recall the other word. However, some of these were incidental-learning experiments: the subjects were asked to process the pairs of words in particular ways but were not told that they would subsequently be tested on their memory for the pairs. Marschark and Hunt showed that effects of imageability would be obtained when the subjects engaged in activities that related together the words in each pair, such as rating how easily two words could be combined into a single unit or how much two words were associated with each other. However, there was no effect of imageability when the subjects were asked to rate the imageability of each word in isolation. In the latter situation, high-imagery words were subsequently remembered no better than low-imagery words. These results show that the use of imagery at the time of presentation is neither necessary nor sufficient to produce effects of imageability.

In another experiment, Marschark and Hunt asked subjects to think of a third word that would help them to remember each pair. For instance, when presented with the pair *microscope–tweezers*, one subject suggested the word "small". If the subjects were subsequently tested with these generated cues, they remembered more high-imagery words than low-imagery words. However, if instead they were tested with one of the words originally presented in each pair, they were no more likely to remember high-imagery words than low-imagery words. These results showed that effects of imageability occurred only when the subjects had engaged in relational processing at the time of presentation (rather than in processing that was specific to the individual items) and when a cue appropriate to the encoded relationship was provided at the time of the retention test.

In some of their experiments, Marschark and Hunt also tested some of their subjects using free recall: in other words, they were simply asked to recall as many of the words as they could without any cues. They found that high-imagery words were better remembered than low-imagery words when the subjects had been asked to rate how easily the words in each pair could be combined into a single unit. However, there was no effect of imageability when the subjects were asked to rate the imageability of each word in isolation, and no effect when the subjects had simply been asked to learn each pair of words without any further instructions. This supported the notion that effects of imageability required relatively extensive relational processing at the time of encoding.

Marschark and Surian (1992) explored the effects of imageability in two incidental-learning experiments in which subjects processed lists of words in different ways and were then unexpectedly given a test of free recall. They showed that there was no effect of imageability on recall performance when the subjects had been asked to rate the imageability of each word in isolation, but that high-imagery words were remembered better than low-imagery words when the subjects had been asked to assign the words to *ad hoc* categories (red things, wooden things, metal things, scientific concepts, religious concepts, and political concepts). However, the effect disappeared when the subjects had been asked to assign a taxonomically structured list of words to genuine categories (fruits, insects, musical instruments, units of time, sciences, and elements). This suggests that the use of imagery as an organisational principle is abolished if other organisational schemes are available, as in Marschark's (1985) experiments on text processing.

This account of effects of imageability is also consistent with the findings mentioned in the previous section. To begin with, it is known that head-injured patients are impaired, not just in their memory performance, but on measures of relational organisation such as categorical clustering (Levin & Goldstein, 1986). Consequently, the framework devised by Marschark et al. (1987) would predict that the memory impairment that is shown by head-injured patients would be more pronounced in the case of high-imagery materials than in the case of low-imagery materials, and hence that the effect of imageability would be reduced or abolished altogether following closed head injury.

In the case of patients who have Huntington's disease and normal volunteers who have received intravenous hyoscine, the effects of imageability may be absent, but only when they are tested using the selective reminding procedure. You may recall that, in this procedure, the subjects are tested over several trials, but only those items that are not recalled on a given trial are presented again for learning on the subsequent trial. This means that the subjects are being continually challenged: on the one hand, on each trial they are required to learn those items which could not be assimilated into the organisational structures that the subjects had previously developed; on the other hand, the subjects are required to do this without any contextual support from items that could be thus assimilated. This continual subversion of the subjects' attempts to achieve a coherent organisation would be particularly devastating when their performance was poor and consequently greater numbers of previously unrecalled items were being presented for relearning on subsequent trials. It follows that the selective reminding procedure is precisely the kind of manipulation which might tend to disrupt relational processing at the time of encoding in individuals with impaired memory function following either brain damage or the administration of psychoactive drugs.

Summary: Imagery as a stimulus attribute

1. Items rated as high imagery are better remembered than items rated as low imagery over a variety of tasks. The effect can be

disrupted by irrelevant visual stimuli, and it cannot be attributed to purely linguistic properties of the materials.

2. The effect of imageability is associated with bilateral activation of the cerebral hemispheres and is found in patients with damage localised within either hemisphere. Hence, it seems to be the result of mechanisms within both hemispheres.

3. The effect is abolished in head-injured patients, and in patients with Huntington's disease and in normal subjects who have received hyoscine when tested by the selective reminding procedure. It can be abolished in normal people by preventing them from using encoded relations or else by providing them with another basis for encoding relational information.

4. The effect was originally taken as evidence for a dual coding theory that was based upon images and verbal representations. However, subsequent evidence is somewhat more consistent with the hypothesis that high-imagery and low-imagery materials differ in terms of the various kinds of relational and distinctive processing that generally occur at the time of encoding, most notably (although not necessarily) in terms of the use of mental imagery.

Imagery as a mnemonic strategy 5

In Chapter 4, I pointed out that the imageability of material was normally (though not inevitably) highly correlated with its memorability. Indeed, one of the key achievements of Paivio's (1971, Chapter 7) early research was to show that imageability was a far better predictor of memory performance in tasks which involve the learning of individual items than any of the other properties that psychologists had previously considered. The evidence is consistent with the notion that the image-evoking potential of material is directly implicated in the mechanisms responsible for learning and remembering.

From this notion, it is only a short step to the idea that it is the actual process of constructing images that gives rise to more effective performance in memory tasks. In other words, mental imagery should be counted amongst the different forms of cognitive processing that determine how effectively information can be remembered. In contemporary cognitive psychology, these cognitive processes are generally thought to be under strategic control and available to conscious introspection. It follows that they can be studied by asking people to describe how they would set about or have set about particular learning tasks.

Accounts of this sort are of interest in their own right, and I shall devote the first part of this chapter to describing research into the cognitive styles and memory strategies which people spontaneously report. However, contemporary notions in cognitive psychology also predict that cognitive processes can be manipulated by giving experimental subjects instructions to set about learning in different ways. The second part of this chapter will therefore examine the effects of such instructions in terms of the use of different learning strategies. Reports of the sort that I have described provide a means of checking whether people have actually complied with their instructions.

In two senses, then, I shall be concerned with imagery as a *mnemonic* strategy. The word "mnemonic" used as an adjective can mean either "pertaining to memory" (as in the first part of this chapter) or "pertaining to the improvement of memory" (as in the second part). When used as a noun, "mnemonic" means "a device or system for improving memory", and I shall also refer to the effectiveness of the classical mnemonics, many of which originated more than 2000 years ago in the times of the ancient Greeks and Romans.

Visualisers and verbalisers

One of the first psychologists to relate memory performance to people's learning strategies was Bartlett (1932, pp. 59–61, 109–112). He found that he could classify his subjects on the basis of their informal comments either as "visualisers", who claimed to rely mainly upon visual imagery in remembering, or as "vocalisers", who claimed to rely mainly upon language cues rather than mental images. Although the vocalisers tended to be less confident in their recall, the two groups produced comparable levels of memory performance. Bartlett suggested that individual people tended to adopt the same approach to remembering across different experiments, and therefore the distinction between "verbalisers" and "visualisers" came to be regarded as reflecting a relatively stable characteristic of individuals or, in other words, a dimension of *cognitive style*. However, the procedures that Bartlett used were rather peculiar by today's standards (involving, for instance, the learning of arbitrary associations between words and simple figures), and different results might be obtained in more conventional tasks.

Paivio (1971, pp. 495–496) devised an instrument which became known as the Individual Difference Questionnaire (IDQ). (It is sometimes called the "Ways of Thinking" questionnaire.) This assessed the degree to which different people habitually used forms of thinking based upon imagery or verbal processes. It contains 86 statements, selected on a purely intuitive basis, to which subjects respond by indicating whether each is true or false of their characteristic ways of thinking, studying, and problem solving (see Paivio & Harshman, 1983, for the full list of statements). Roughly half the items are positively worded statements, while the others are negatively worded to control for any general tendency on the subject's part simply to agree or disagree regardless of the content of the items themselves.

The IDQ contains 39 items intended to measure the strength of people's preference for using visual imagery; these include the following examples:

- I often use mental pictures to solve problems.
- I can easily picture moving objects in my mind.
- I can add numbers by imagining them to be written on a blackboard.
- I find it difficult to form a mental picture of anything.

The IDQ also contains 47 items intended to measure the strength of people's preference for using verbal thinking; these include the following examples:

- I enjoy doing work that requires the use of words.
- Most of the time my thinking is verbal, as though talking to myself.
- I enjoy solving crossword puzzles and other word games.
- I have difficulty producing associations for words.

Paivio administered the IDQ to 96 students, together with a battery of other questionnaires and psychological tests which included the Minnesota Paper Form Board (MPFB), a commonly used test of spatial ability, and the questionnaire that was devised by Barratt (1953) to assess the imagery that people experienced while carrying out the MPFB. (This questionnaire was discussed in Chapter 3.) The application of factor analysis to the data showed that the imagery score on the IDQ generated its highest loading on the same factor as the questionnaire concerning the MPFB; this factor also showed loadings on a version of Galton's (1880) breakfast-table questionnaire and Sheehan's (1967a) shortened form of the Questionnaire upon Mental Imagery (QMI) (see Chapter 2), as well as the subjects' actual performance on the MPFB. In contrast, the verbal score on the IDQ generated its highest loading on the same factor as a vocabulary test. Very similar findings were obtained in subsequent research carried out by A. Richardson (1977a) and by Hiscock (1978).

Hiscock (1976, 1978) dropped 15 items from the IDQ because they were not sufficiently correlated with the total scores on the relevant scale (in other words, the total imagery score or the total verbal score). He then added one new item and changed the response categories from true-or-false to a 5-point scale. Hiscock found that his reduced, 72-item version of the IDQ had satisfactory levels of internal consistency and test–retest reliability. (See Chapter 2 for an explanation of these properties of questionnaires.) Hiscock categorised 40 subjects as visualisers or verbalisers by comparing the visual and verbal scores that they obtained on the 72-item version of the IDQ. They were then tested on the recall of adjectives and nouns from a narrative passage containing either high-imagery or low-imagery adjectives. (The imageability of the nouns was not specified, but it can be assumed that they were at least moderately imageable so that they could sensibly be modified by high-imagery adjectives.) The verbalisers recalled more nouns from the passage than the visualisers, and they also tended to recall more low-imagery adjectives. However, the visualisers recalled more high-imagery adjectives than the verbalisers.

Hiscock (1978) found that the imagery and verbal scales within the original, 86-item IDQ appeared to have satisfactory internal consistency. However, when Paivio and Harshman (1983) carried out factor analyses on the responses that were given to the individual items, they identified an imagery factor and a verbal factor, but also a number of more specific factors. In other words, the IDQ does not appear to be a "pure" measure of the habitual use of imagery and verbal processes as Paivio had originally intended. This conclusion probably applies to the shorter, 72-item version developed by Hiscock as well.

B.H. Cohen and Saslona (1990) devised an "imagery habit scale" (IDQ-IHS) on the basis of 12 of the items that loaded most highly on the imagery factor which had been identified by Paivio and Harshman (1983), and like Hiscock (1978) they changed the response format to a 5-point scale. This revised instrument was claimed to have satisfactory levels of internal consistency and test–retest reliability. Cohen and Saslona found that it predicted performance on an intentional memory test for pictured objects and on an incidental memory test for their colours. In contrast, they found that scores on Marks's (1973) Vividness of Visual Imagery Questionnaire were unrelated to scores on the IDQ-IHS and did not reliably predict memory for the objects and their colours.

In a similar manner, Weatherly, Ball, and Stacks (1997) selected 10 items from the imagery factor identified by Paivio and Harshman (1983) and used them as the basis for a measure of the habitual use of visual imagery. Those subjects who reported a greater habitual use of imagery also achieved a significantly higher level of accuracy on a test of mental rotation involving two-dimensional shapes. However, the subjects' habitual use of imagery was not related to their response latencies or to their reports of the strategies that they had used to carry out this task. In addition, the effect on accuracy became non-significant with practice as the level of performance approached a ceiling.

Paivio and Harshman (1983) found no significant difference between men and women with regard to their tendency to endorse the items on the imagery scale of the original IDQ. However, Hiscock (1978) and Ernest (1983) both found that women achieved significantly higher scores than men on this scale. Harshman and Paivio (1987) pointed out that the items in the IDQ were randomly ordered and specifically designed to counterbalance positively worded items against negatively worded ones. They therefore argued that these gender differences were a genuine phenomenon and not merely the result of a more lenient response bias on the part of women. They suggested that by implication analogous gender differences found by other researchers on the shortened form of the QMI (see Chapter 2) were also not likely to be the result of a response bias.

On inspection of the responses given by men and women to individual items in the IDQ, Harshman and Paivio found that women were more likely than men to report the use of imagery in remembering, the evocation of mental images of previously experienced scenes, and the spontaneous arousal of imagery by verbal stimuli. For instance, women were more likely than men to endorse the following items:

- I often remember work I have studied by imagining the page on which it is written.
- When reading fiction I usually form a mental picture of a scene or room that has been described.

In contrast, men were more likely than women to report the use of imagery in problem solving and to report the ability to visualise moving objects. For instance, men were more likely than women to endorse the following items:

- I can easily picture moving objects in my mind.
- By using mental pictures of the elements of a problem, I am often able to arrive at a solution.

Harshman and Paivio concluded "that females may excel more frequently at static memory imagery, whereas males may excel more frequently at dynamic transformation or manipulation of images" (p. 287).

Subsequently, Paivio and Clark (1991) pointed out that these findings were consistent with the general tendency for women to report more vivid imagery than men (see Chapter 2) and with the general tendency for men to outperform women on tests of spatial ability (see Chapter 3). They went on to show that men produced faster response times than women when they were asked to generate dynamic images but that women produced faster response times than men when they were asked to generate static images. You might remember from Chapter 3 that a functional distinction is widely accepted in contemporary discussions of visuo-spatial working memory between a passive short-term store or visual buffer and an active process of spatial rehearsal and transformation (see Kosslyn, 1980, 1994; Logie, 1995). These findings suggest that women tend to be more efficient than men in the generation and maintenance of information in the passive visual store, whereas men tend to be more efficient than women in the manipulation and transformation of that information.

Visualisers, verbalisers, and hemispheric asymmetry

It was fairly inevitable that the supposed cognitive style that distinguished verbalisers from visualisers should eventually be linked to the functional asymmetry between the left and right hemispheres of the brain (see Chapter 1). However, lacking the brain-imaging technology that is available today, researchers had to look for some kind of behavioural marker of processing in the brain.

In the early 1970s, the results of two different studies suggested that people tended to shift the direction of their gaze to the right when they were trying to answer verbal questions (such as "Define the word *economics*"), but that they tended to shift the direction of their gaze to the left when trying to answer visual or spatial questions (such as "Which way does George Washington's head face on a quarter?") (Kinsbourne, 1972; Kocel, Galin, Ornstein, & Merrin, 1972). Presuming that eye movements to one side or the other might be initiated by an increase in the level of activation of the opposite hemisphere, this phenomenon was speculatively linked to the notion that the left hemisphere was specialised for verbal processing while the right hemisphere was specialised for visuo-spatial processing. Nevertheless, it was also noticed that there were consistent individual differences in lateral eye movements, so that some people habitually shifted their gaze to the left, while others habitually shifted their gaze to the right. This phenomenon, too, was linked to variation in the activation of the opposite hemisphere (see also Bakan, 1969; Bakan & Strayer, 1973).

A. Richardson (1977b) tested 44 high-school girls on five verbal questions and five visual questions, and found that 17 responded with leftward eye movements on eight or more of the questions, whereas 14 responded with rightward eye movements on eight or more of the questions. He had previously administered Paivio's (1971) IDQ to these subjects, and the two subgroups showed statistically significant differences on nine of the items in the IDQ and marginally significant differences on two others. In each case, the subgroup who tended to shift their gaze to the left were more likely to give responses indicative of imagery, whereas the subgroup who tended to shift their gaze to the right were more likely to give responses indicative of verbal processing.

Richardson added a further four items to these 11 items to yield a new instrument, the Verbaliser–Visualiser Questionnaire (VVQ). Each of the original subjects was then assigned a score equal to the total number of responses indicative of the use of imagery rather than verbal processing. Not surprisingly, this score was found to be highly correlated with the number of leftward eye movements made to the test questions across the entire group of 44 girls. Again unsurprisingly (since the VVQ is a subset of the IDQ), Richardson showed in another group of subjects that scores on the VVQ were positively related to imagery scores on the IDQ and to vividness ratings on the short form of the QMI, and negatively related to verbal scores on the IDQ and to scores on a vocabulary test.

Richardson himself found that the test–retest reliability of the VVQ was very high, but measures from subsequent research have been much lower. Applications of factor analysis have identified anywhere between two and six factors underlying the VVQ, and its internal consistency is correspondingly poor (see A. Richardson, 1994, p. 37). Several studies have now found that VVQ scores are positively but weakly related to ratings of the vividness or controllability of experienced imagery, negatively related to scores on vocabulary tests and other measures of verbal aptitude, but essentially unrelated to scores on tests of spatial ability and other aspects of cognitive performance (Alesandrini, 1981; Edwards & Wilkins, 1981; Green & Schroeder, 1990; Kirby, Moore, & Schofield, 1988; Parrott, 1986; but cf. Poltrock & Brown, 1984). These findings imply that the VVQ is a very heterogeneous instrument that is not measuring a single unidimensional construct of cognitive style as Richardson had originally intended.

At the same time, it is highly unlikely that the initial rationale for the VVQ can be sustained. Experiments carried out during the 1970s indicated that lateral eye movements could be highly inconsistent and could be influenced by a number of extraneous variables (see Berg & Harris, 1980; A. Richardson, 1978). Indeed, when A. Richardson (1977b) tried to replicate his original experiment with a sample of 102 university students, their VVQ scores were *negatively* related to the number of leftward eye movements made to the 10 test questions. He duly found that seven subjects responded with leftward eye movements on eight or more of the questions, and that 21 responded with rightward eye movements on eight or more of the questions. However, the former subgroup were actually *less* likely than the latter to produce responses indicative of the use of imagery on 11 out of the 15 items in the VVQ. Parrott (1986) found no relation at all between VVQ scores and lateral eye movements.

In short, careful research has essentially discredited the idea that lateral eye movements could be taken as indicators of relative hemispheric activation in response to test questions, although *spontaneous* eye movements do appear to be related to gross hemispheric activity: if the activity within one cerebral hemisphere is suppressed by the injection of sodium amytal into one carotid artery, the patient's spontaneous gaze is likely to deviate to the same side as the injection (Meador, Loring, Lee, Brooks, Nichols, Thompson, Thompson, & Heilman, 1989). There is in any case very little independent evidence that the questions administered to subjects in the original studies did in fact activate the hemispheres in the manner that they were supposed to (see Ehrlichman & Weinberger, 1978). Indeed, I pointed out in Chapters 2 and 3 that instructions to experimental subjects to make up mental images and experimental tasks that involve image generation may well implicate anatomical regions in the left hemisphere rather than in the right hemisphere.

Cognitive styles and memory strategies

The results that were obtained by Paivio (1971, pp. 495–496) confirmed that people can give quite useful accounts of their preferred modes of thinking and that these accounts can predict their performance in objective tests (such as the MPFB). However, they also suggest that more accurate predictions can be obtained by asking people to give accounts of the specific modes of thinking that they have used in particular tasks, as in the questionnaire devised by

Barratt (1953). As I mentioned at the beginning of this chapter, these accounts are of considerable interest in their own right, but in experiments that involve instructing different groups of subjects to use different strategies they also provide a means of checking whether they have actually complied with their instructions.

A good illustration of this is a study of imagery and the learning of prose that was described by R.C. Anderson and Kulhavy (1972). They asked two groups of subjects to read a passage of prose about a fictitious primitive tribe and then tested their retention of the information in the passage by a combination of short, open-ended questions and multiple-choice questions. One group was asked to form a vivid mental picture of everything described in the passage, and the other group was simply asked to read the text carefully. However, Anderson and Kulhavy also gave the subjects a questionnaire in which they asked about the study strategies which they had employed in the learning task, their carefulness, and their interest in the materials. They found that more than half of the control group had used mental imagery while studying the prose passage without having been instructed to do so, whereas a third of the experimental group who were instructed to use imagery reported that they had not done so or had done so only at the beginning of the passage.

In a subsequent study, McDaniel and Kearney (1984) asked subjects to carry out three different learning tasks under various instructions and then asked them to describe how often they had used different strategies. One task involved the free recall of a list which contained three words from each of 11 semantic categories; the second task involved the cued recall of 32 paired associates containing high-imagery nouns; and the third task involved recalling the definitions of 15 unfamiliar words. Different groups of subjects were instructed to carry out these tasks using an image, a sentence, or a superordinate category for each item to be remembered. A fourth group was simply asked to carry out any mental operations that they thought would be useful in learning the materials.

McDaniel and Kearney found that the most efficient strategy varied from one task to another. All three sets of instructions were equally effective on the free-recall task; the imagery and sentence instructions were more effective than the category instructions on the paired-associate task; and the imagery instructions were more effective than the sentence or category instructions on the vocabulary task. Moreover, the uninstructed subjects tended spontaneously to use the most efficient strategy or strategies for each learning task. As a consequence, they performed at least as well as any of the instructed groups on the free-recall task and the vocabulary task, although they did less well than the subjects who were given imagery or sentence instructions on the paired-associate task. McDaniel and Kearney concluded that the effectiveness of particular memory strategies depended on whether they promoted the encoding of requisite information that was not activated spontaneously by the material to be learned itself; conversely, if the material spontaneously activates an effective strategy, then giving the subjects different instructions as to how to set about the task is likely to prove largely ineffective.

This was confirmed in a study by McDougall and Velmans (1993), who asked subjects to learn pairs of words describing objects that normally occur in spatial contiguity (such as *flag–mast*) or pairs of words drawn from the same taxonomic category (such as *potato–spinach*). They found that subjects usually reported using imagery to learn the former pairs and using verbal strategies to learn the latter pairs. Giving the subjects explicit instructions either to use imagery or to use a verbal strategy had no effect upon the strategies that were actually used and had no effect upon the subjects' performance. An important feature of McDougall and Velmans' research is that these effects were obtained even when pairs of both types were presented in a random sequence within a single list. As they concluded, their subjects were apparently able to adjust their strategies from one pair of words to the next in a dynamic and flexible manner in accordance with the specific nature of the relation within each pair. In short, the distinction between imaginal and verbal coding appears to relate more to optional strategies that could be used within the same subject than to cognitive styles that distinguish between different subjects.

The results obtained by McDougall and Velmans confirm the finding of R.C. Anderson and Kulhavy (1972) that for whatever reason subjects taking part in memory experiments do not always comply with explicit instructions. This has also been noted in other cognitive tasks such as sentence–picture verification (Marquer & Pereira, 1990). This led Ericsson and Simon (1993, p. lii) to argue that it was essential in any cognitive research to obtain some form of report to assess the strategies that were actually being adopted by individual subjects. Nevertheless, in obtaining accounts from their subjects as to how they had set about their respective learning tasks, R.C. Anderson and Kulhavy (1972) and McDaniel and Kearney (1984) posed relatively general questions about how often they had used particular strategies. Ericsson and Simon suggested that subjects might sometimes have difficulty in responding to queries at such a general level and that they would therefore resort to inferences and speculation when generating their accounts (p. xlix). Other researchers have shown that accurate accounts of cognitive processing can only be obtained through specific questions which reflect the subjects' ongoing cognitive activities and serve to reinstate the context in which the processing actually occurred (Cantor, Andreassen, & Waters, 1985; Hoc & Leplat, 1983). Ericsson and Simon therefore concluded that more valid information could be obtained by cueing the subjects with specific items taken from the original experiment (p. xlix).

Reported mediators in associative learning

One of the earliest studies to collect accounts of this sort was described by Reed (1918). He asked 27 subjects to learn four sets of paired associates: two sets consisted of unrelated pairs of English words (such as *sauce–balloon, radish–coffee*); the third consisted of German words paired with their English translations (such as *Wipfel–summit*); and the fourth contained pairs of consonant-vowel-consonant (CVC) nonsense syllables (such as *wum–pir*). (The subjects were apparently unfamiliar with German.) When Reed asked his subjects how they had tried to remember the pairs of English words, they tended to report associative aids based upon shared semantic features (e.g. *simmer–tarry*, "Both slow") or upon linking images or phrases (e.g. *ring–kitten*, "A ring around a kitten's neck"). However, in the case of the other pairs, they were more likely to report the use of linking words that were similar to the sounds of the words in each pair (e.g. *heb–tup*, "Head top").

Reed noted that every subject reported that some paired associates had been learned with the use of these associative aids, but that others had been learned "mechanically, i.e., without association" (p. 133). He then demonstrated that on each set of paired associates reports of associative aids were linked to better recall during the original learning phase and better retention when the subjects were retested the following day. Reed concluded that these findings established a causal relationship between the use of associative aids and the rates with which learning and forgetting occurred. Because these associative aids *mediate* (or serve as intermediaries) between the items that have to be remembered, they are often nowadays described as "mediators".

Unfortunately, the publication of Reed's article happened to coincide with the rise of the behaviourist movement (see Chapter 2). Consequently, the idea of asking subjects how they had set about particular memory tasks was very much discouraged until the advent of modern cognitive psychology in the 1960s. Even then, few researchers bothered to ask their subjects what they were actually doing in their experiments, and those who did were very tentative in the conclusions they were prepared to reach. This somewhat timid approach to the collection of subjects' accounts is well illustrated in the following remarks from an article by Runquist and Farley (1964):

> When Ss [subjects] are asked how they learn verbal paired-associate lists, they inevitably claim to use some kind of mediator, either another word or several words, an image, or other mnemonic device of some kind. Although it usually is considered dangerous to treat these utterances as having any scientific importance, the ubiquity of the reports of mediators seems to warrant their investigation. (p. 280)

Nevertheless, during the 1960s, several researchers confirmed Reed's findings that associative aids were commonly reported in verbal-learning tasks and that pairs learned with the use of associative aids were remembered better than pairs learned without their use (see Paivio, 1971, Chapter 9). These studies involved paired associates consisting of letters and numbers; random letter trigrams and common three-letter words; pairs of CVC nonsense syllables; or CVC nonsense syllables and words.

Martin, Boersma, and Cox (1965) classified the reports given by subjects learning pairs of bisyllabic non-words (e.g. *latuk–brugen*). They identified five categories of associative devices, plus repetition (i.e. rote rehearsal) and no reported association. They tested their subjects using a recognition procedure and found that the number of correct responses given during the learning of each pair was associated with the apparent complexity of the corresponding reported mediator; in particular, performance was good with associative devices, intermediate with repetition, and poor when subjects reported no association at all.

Experiments which used pairs of words (such as pairs of adjectives) tended to produce reports of associative mediators consisting chiefly of simple sentences linking the two words in each pair. Runquist and Farley (1964) gave the example, "The *classic* complexion has a *ruddy* look" (p. 283). These findings were interpreted as evidence for the importance of *natural language mediation* in verbal learning: in other words, the subjects were using familiar expressions from everyday language to solve the problem of finding some device for connecting two items together. In addition, other researchers demonstrated that improved performance would be obtained if simple linking sentences were provided by the experimenter, and that an even greater amount of improvement could result if the subjects were instructed to make up such sentences for themselves (see, for example, Bobrow & Bower, 1969).

However, the research on natural language mediators was limited in two different ways. First, the researchers allowed their subjects to describe the mediators they had used in an open-ended fashion, which made it difficult to achieve any coherent classification of different devices without resorting to *ad hoc* schemes of the sort devised by Martin et al. (1965). It might be advantageous to require the subjects to give their reports within some *a priori* classification scheme so that they could more easily be compared and quantified. Second, Runquist and Farley (1964) specifically referred to the use of imagery as a mediating device in the passage that I quoted above, yet images were virtually never mentioned in the accounts collected by researchers interested in natural language mediation. In retrospect, the overwhelming predominance of verbal mediators in these early studies seems to have been due mainly to the use of relatively meaningless or abstract materials.

Mental imagery as a mediating device

Paivio, Yuille, and Smythe (1966) collected mediator reports following the presentation of a list of paired associates for four learning trials. The materials were nouns selected in order to vary imageability, concreteness, and meaningfulness. Instead of asking the subjects open-ended questions, Paivio et al. administered post-learning questionnaires in which the subjects were asked to report whether they had learned each paired associate by using a verbal mediator (such as a phrase or rhyme connecting the two words), by making up a mental image (such as a mental "picture" which included the two items), or without using any such device. Verbal mediators were reported for 40% of abstract, low-imagery pairs, but for only 15% of concrete, high-imagery pairs. Conversely, imaginal mediators were reported for 59% of concrete, high-imagery pairs, but for only 19% of abstract, low-imagery pairs.

As well as studying the *availability* of mediators of these different types, measured by the unconditional probability that mediators of any particular type would be reported, Paivio et al. assessed the *effectiveness* of mediators of different types, measured by the conditional probability that a paired associate would be correctly recalled, given that a mediator of each type had been reported. In agreement with Reed (1918) and with the research on natural language mediators, those pairs for which mediators were reported were more likely to be remembered than pairs for which mediators were not reported. Both imaginal mediators and verbal mediators appeared to be more effective when learning high-imagery pairs than when learning low-imagery pairs. In addition, imaginal mediators seemed to be more effective than verbal mediators, but only when learning high-imagery pairs, not when learning low-imagery pairs.

These findings encouraged Paivio and Yuille (1967) to collect mediator reports in a further experiment in which the subjects were specifically instructed to use verbal mediators, mental imagery, or rote repetition in order to learn materials varying in either imageability or meaningfulness. Afterwards, the subjects were asked to report whether they had in fact tried to learn each pair by repetition, verbal mediation, imaginal mediation, some other device, or no such strategy. The subjects who had been instructed to use verbal mediators or mental imagery achieved higher recall scores than the subjects who had been instructed to use rote repetition. In addition, an analysis of the mediator reports showed that these varied among the three groups in accordance with their instructions.

However, Paivio and Yuille found that the distribution of reported mediators was determined more by the properties of the pairs being learned than by the particular instructions under which the pairs had been learned. For instance, the subjects who had received imagery instructions reported that they had in fact used imaginal mediators for 82% of high-imagery pairs but only 28% of low-imagery pairs. Similar results were obtained by Paivio and Yuille (1969), who showed that imaginal mediators (and to some extent verbal mediators, too) were reported more often over successive learning trials, quite regardless of the instructions that had been given. As Paivio (1971, p. 362) later commented, these results demonstrated that subjects' associative strategies were only partly controlled by their experimental instructions and might often be determined more by the semantic properties of the materials to be remembered. Similar results were obtained in the studies by

McDaniel and Kearney (1984) and by McDougall and Velmans (1993) that I mentioned earlier in this chapter.

One possible implication of the results obtained by Paivio et al. (1966) is that it should be possible to predict the memory performance of individual subjects on the basis of their reported use of imaginal and verbal mediators. I examined this idea in an experiment on paired-associate learning (J.T.E. Richardson, 1978b). I considered various possible measures of the use of mental imagery, but the best predictor of recall performance across different subjects was simply the total number of pairs for which each subject reported having used an imaginal mediator. (The correlation coefficient was +0.80, which means that 64% of the variation in performance could be explained by variation in the use of imagery.) A subsequent experiment showed that this relationship applied in the case of high-imagery pairs, but not in the case of low-imagery pairs.

The effects of imagery instructions

The efficacy of instructions and training in the use of mental imagery has been known about more generally for a long time. Various techniques prescribed for orators in Greek and Roman times included the explicit use of imagery (see Paivio, 1971, Chapter 6; Yates, 1966). Such techniques or *mnemonics* were very important because the ability to deliver convincing speeches in public without reference to written notes was highly valued. Mnemonics were therefore significant in the art of rhetoric (or persuasive speaking), although Aristotle thought that they were useful for remembering general patterns of argument and could therefore be important in dialectic (or logical debating), too (Sorabji, 1972, pp. 27–31). These techniques have survived largely unchanged to the present day in the courses of memory improvement regularly advertised in newspapers and magazines.

Experimental research on the efficacy of instructions to subjects to use mental imagery in learning verbal material has generally demonstrated consistent, reliable, and substantial improvements in performance. These effects have been found when retention is tested using free recall (i.e. recalling the items in any order), serial recall (i.e. recalling the items in the original order of presentation), the cued recall of paired associates, and recognition. They have been demonstrated when comparisons are made between groups of subjects given different learning instructions, when comparisons are made within a group of subjects before and after they are given instructions to use mental imagery, and even when comparisons are made between different items that are being learned simultaneously by the same subjects (see J.T.E. Richardson, 1980b, p. 70). Nevertheless, instructions to use mental imagery usually lead to improved recall only in the case of high-imagery material, not in the case of low-imagery material (see J.T.E. Richardson, 1980b, p. 95).

In laboratory experiments, it is usually sufficient to ask the subjects merely to construct mental images that link the items to be remembered together in some way. (The "linking" is an important feature that will be discussed in more detail in a moment.) However, traditional mnemonic systems often involved providing far more structure for the material to be remembered. For example, using the method of loci (or place mnemonic), the subjects learn a sequence of items by constructing an image locating each object at a particular location on a well-known route (for example, a walk around their own neighbourhood or their college campus). The items can then be recalled by mentally repeating the walk and retrieving the object at each location.

Similarly, using the "one–bun" mnemonic (or "pegword mnemonic"), the subjects learn the following nonsense rhyme:

> One is a bun,
> two is a shoe,
> three is a tree,
> four is a door,
> five is a hive,
> six is sticks,
> seven is heaven,
> eight is a gate,
> nine is wine,
> ten is a hen.

This can then be used to learn a sequence of items by making up a compound image relating the first object and a bun, another image relating the second object and a shoe, and so on. The items can be retrieved by rehearsing the rhyme and retrieving the object associated with each of the "pegs" or cue words.

One of the traditional elements of techniques for the improvement of memory is the prescription that the learner should try to produce images that are in some way bizarre or peculiar. Instructions to produce bizarre images have been found to produce increased recall performance when compared with standard learning instructions that do not specify any particular learning strategy. However, studies that have attempted to separate the effect of bizarreness from the effect of imaging *per se* have failed to find any additional effect of constructing bizarre images over and above the benefit of using mental imagery. Indeed, bizarre images tend to take longer to construct than images depicting more conventional or plausible situations and may result in poorer performance. Bizarreness is thus not a very important factor determining the beneficial effects of imagery in learning and remembering (see J.T.E. Richardson, 1980b, pp. 72–73; cf. Einstein & McDaniel, 1987).

It is possible, in principle, that all these effects are attributable to other factors and are not specifically due to the use of imagery. The most plausible alternative explanation is that instructions to use imagery simply boost the subjects' motivation to learn. The most crucial difficulty for this sort of account is that instructions to make up mental images of the material being presented are just as effective in experiments on incidental learning, in which the subjects are unaware that their retention of that material will subsequently be tested (see Bower, 1972; Paivio, 1969). Indeed, imagery instructions tend to enhance performance on high-imagery material, as I mentioned above, whereas instructions to motivate the subjects to learn tend to enhance performance on low-imagery material (Sheehan, 1972). Another consideration is that subjects' reports of their use of imaginal mediators increase in response to imagery instructions in a manner that is concomitant with the level of their recall performance (Paivio & Yuille, 1967).

Nevertheless, motivational factors may well explain two otherwise puzzling findings from my own research concerning the effectiveness of imagery instructions. Both findings emerged in the further analysis of results obtained when investigating the effects of closed head injury (see below), but they were equally apparent in the data obtained from control patients and do not seem to have an intrinsic connection with head injuries. First, middle-class patients benefited from these instructions but working-class patients did not, at least when tested by a middle-class psychologist (J.T.E. Richardson, 1987). Second, and independent of the first effect, the benefits of imagery instructions declined consistently with age from the teens to the sixties, at least when the patients were tested by a young adult psychologist (J.T.E. Richardson & Rossan, 1994). This pattern of results is quite unlike most effects of ageing on cognitive functioning, which are normally not apparent until the fifties or sixties. Both findings can more plausibly be interpreted in terms of variations in perceived demand characteristics: in other words, the patients were led to take the task more or less seriously, depending upon whether the tester was perceived to be like or unlike themselves in age and social class.

Paivio (1971) himself explained the effectiveness of imagery instructions in terms of his dual coding theory and the coding redundancy hypothesis which were mentioned in Chapter 4. According to this explanation, recall performance varies with the number of alternative memory codes available for an item:

> Any superiority observed under imagery mnemonic conditions may result from the addition of imagery to a verbal baseline laid down during the subject's initial representational or associative reactions to the to-be-learned items, i.e., two mediational systems are potentially available rather than one. (p. 389)

Presumably, the effective use of imagery mnemonics depends upon the use of visuo-spatial working memory. Consistent with this idea, Di Vesta and Sunshine (1974) found that people of high spatial ability produced better memory performance than people of low spatial ability when they were using the pegword mnemonic, but not when given verbal mediation instructions. As I mentioned in Chapter 4, Paivio (1972) noted that increasing the presentation rate was one way of selectively interfering with cognitive processing. The fact that imagery instructions are more effective at slower rates of presentation (see Paivio, 1971, pp. 343–344) could thus be taken as evidence that imagery instructions involve additional forms of processing in memory.

However, it should be possible selectively to disrupt the improvement gained from the use of imagery mnemonics by making subjects carry out concurrent visuo-spatial tasks. During the 1970s, a number of investigators examined this possibility, but they regularly failed to show that concurrent visuo-spatial tasks disrupted the benefits of imagery instructions (see J.T.E. Richardson, 1980b, pp. 78–79). One possible explanation for this is that the cognitive demands of creating an elaborative image linking two separate items are relatively minimal and can therefore be readily accommodated at the same time as tasks which impose a greater load on subjects' processing capacity.

Baddeley and Lieberman (1980) investigated the effects of a concurrent tracking task upon the retention of sequences of items. They found that the advantage of using the "one–bun" mnemonic was slightly reduced when the subjects were required to perform a concurrent tracking task. Similarly, Logie (1986) showed that the concurrent presentation of irrelevant visual materials (such as patterns or pictures) impaired performance if subjects were using the pegword mnemonic, but not when they were using rote repetition; conversely, the concurrent presentation of irrelevant speech disrupted performance when the subjects were using rote repetition but not when they were using the pegword mnemonic.

These results suggest that concurrent visuo-spatial tasks selectively disrupt the use of more complex imagery mnemonics (see also Quinn & McConnell, 1996). Indeed, in a further study, Baddeley and Lieberman found that the usefulness of the method of loci was drastically reduced when subjects were required to carry out a concurrent tracking task. Moreover, Cornoldi and De Beni (1991) found that the method of loci could be more helpful when learning orally presented text than when learning written text. This finding was replicated by De Beni, Moè, and Cornoldi (1997), who claimed that having to read the material interfered with the usefulness of mnemonics based upon visual imagery.

Imagery and verbal instructions

Although imagery instructions do often give rise to substantial improvements in memory performance, I pointed out earlier that improvements often also result when subjects are given verbal instructions (that is, instructions to make up linking phrases or sentences). Indeed, many researchers found no significant difference between imagery and verbal instructions in terms of the resulting improvement. However, the results obtained by Paivio and Yuille (1967) showed that it cannot just be assumed that the relevant processing will automatically be induced by instructions to use mental imagery or verbal mediation.

Moreover, experiments of this sort may underestimate the effectiveness of mental imagery as a mnemonic strategy, because many people appear to use mental imagery in learning even when they have not been explicitly instructed to do so. In fact, a study that was carried out with college students found that the effectiveness of imagery instructions was inversely related to their verbal ability (that is, they were least effective in the most able students). This apparently reflected the fact that people of high verbal ability will spontaneously use effective learning strategies (McDaniel & Pressley, 1984).

To try to tackle such problems, Paivio and Foth (1970) carried out an experiment on paired-associate learning in which they forced their subjects to externalise their mental images and verbal mediators in the form of drawn pictures and written phrases or sentences during the 15 seconds in which each pair was presented. They found that imagery instructions yielded better performance than verbal instructions on high-imagery pairs, but poorer performance than verbal instructions on low-imagery pairs. Paivio and Foth had also recorded the times taken by the subjects to begin drawing a picture or to begin writing a phrase or sentence: they found no difference in these response latencies on the high-imagery pairs, but longer latencies for pictures than for verbal mediators on the low-imagery pairs.

Paivio and Foth suggested that the poorer performance on low-imagery pairs under imagery instructions was attributable to the reduced availability of imaginal mediators. Indeed, on average, their subjects had been unable to generate an imaginal mediator for 27% of the low-imagery pairs within the time limit of 15 seconds. Using the same test procedure but with self-paced presentation, Yuille (1973) confirmed that imaginal mediators required longer to produce than did verbal mediators for the low-imagery pairs, but he found that subsequent performance was not significantly different between the two instructional sets. This implies that imaginal and verbal mediators differ in their availability for low-imagery pairs, but that they do not differ in their effectiveness once they have become available.

According to Paivio and Foth's latency data, there seemed to be no difference between the availability of imaginal and verbal mediators for the high-imagery pairs. This indicated that the superior performance obtained on high-imagery pairs under imagery instructions should be attributed to the greater effectiveness of imaginal mediators when learning such pairs. Yuille (1973) confirmed that imaginal mediators were discovered as quickly as verbal mediators for high-imagery pairs. In his experiment, however, imaginal mediators produced better recall than verbal mediators only if the subjects were tested after a one-week delay. On immediate testing, there was no significant difference between recall performance using imaginal and verbal mediators, regardless of the imageability of the materials.

However, the procedure that was adopted by Paivio and Foth is vulnerable to the criticism that it confounded the effects of instructing the subjects to make up a mental image or verbal mediator with the effects of instructing them to draw a picture or to write down a phrase or sentence (Janssen, 1976a). For instance, since the subjects who were instructed to use imagery were effectively being instructed to provide themselves with a pictorial representation of the material to be recalled, it is in principle impossible to determine which of these constituted the effective mnemonic device. It is also conceivable that, in experiments such as these, the subjects will create drawings in order to comply with their instructions even if they have been unable to make up a relevant mental image; in this situation, the drawn picture would in fact be a substitute for an imaginal mediator rather than its visible, objective counterpart.

Interactive and separative instructions

While it has generally been established that instructions to use imagery in learning often lead to substantial improvements in recall and recognition performance, there is one important exception to this generalisation: it is crucial that the mental imagery used by the subjects in such experiments serves to increase the organisation and cohesion of the material to be remembered. Accordingly, instructions to generate separate mental images corresponding to the individual items may have no effect on performance at all, and may even lead to a reduction in the level of recall.

This was first identified in a study by Bower (1972). He compared the incidental-learning performance of a group who had received "interaction" instructions (to make up a mental image depicting two objects interacting in some way) with that of a second group who received "separation" instructions (to make up an image depicting the two objects "separated in their imaginal space, like two pictures on opposite walls of a room"; p. 80). The first group showed the usual marked superiority in recall when they were cued with one of the words in each pair, whereas the second group performed at the level that would be expected under instructions to use rote repetition. As Bower concluded: "Instructions to image the terms *per se* have relatively little effect on associative learning. The important component is the interactive relation between the imaged objects" (p. 80). In another study, Bower (1970) replicated this basic effect using intentional-learning conditions and a control group who were instructed to use overt rote repetition.

Similar findings were obtained in subsequent experiments, although most researchers used slightly different separation instructions in which the subjects were merely told to make up a separate mental image for each individual item. For example, Morris and

Stevens (1974) studied the usefulness of interactive and separative imagery in the free recall of lists consisting of groups of three nouns, and they found that only interaction instructions helped memory performance. This indicates that the pattern observed by Bower (1972) arises not only in associative learning but in other kinds of memory task as well. Morris and Stevens also assessed the subjects' memory organisation of the material by measuring the extent to which the members of each group of nouns tended to be recalled together. They found that differences in recall performance were directly associated with concomitant differences in memory organisation.

As I mentioned in Chapter 4, Marschark and Hunt (1989) showed that there was no difference between the recall of pairs of high-imagery and low-imagery words when the subjects were asked to rate the imageability of each word in isolation and then received an unanticipated test of either free recall or cued recall. Marschark and Surian (1992) obtained very similar results when subjects were presented with lists of unrelated words to be rated on their imageability and then received an unanticipated test of free recall (see also J.T.E. Richardson, 1979a). In fact, this separative imagery manipulation abolished the effect of imageability both on the level of performance and on the level of categorical clustering in free recall. In short, interactive imagery enhances recall, relational organisation, and the effect of imageability; separative imagery does not enhance recall or relational organisation, and it may even eliminate the effect of imageability.

Dual coding or dual processing?

It has been known for many years that organisation is important in verbal learning, and that procedures to enhance organisation which are simply based upon verbal categorisation can also lead to substantial improvements in performance (see, for instance, Mandler, 1967). Consequently, Bower's argument undermined the supposition, central to dual coding theory, that mental imagery gives rise to a qualitatively different form of memory code or representation. Bower (1970, 1972) developed this argument by pointing to parallels between the results obtained in comparing interactive and separative imagery, and the results obtained in comparing the recall of pictures and the recall of word pairs. Previous research had shown that two pictured objects were more easily recalled if they were shown in some sort of interaction. Similarly, it was known that the recall of noun pairs was aided if they were embedded in a meaningful sentence and connected by a verb or proposition. This facilitation did not occur if the sentence was anomalous (in which case performance may actually be reduced) or when the two nouns were connected merely by a conjunction (e.g. Bobrow & Bower, 1969; Rohwer, 1966).

On the basis of the similarities among these experimental results, Bower (1972) concluded that "this recall pattern with pictures, images, and words is probably being produced by the same relational generating system" (p. 81). Other researchers tended to agree with the notion that both imaginal and verbal instructions simply encouraged the relational organisation of the material to be remembered within a single code or system (J.R. Anderson & Bower, 1973, p. 457; Begg, 1978; Rohwer, 1973). In Chapter 4, I referred to the argument which was put forward by Marschark, Richman, Yuille, and Hunt (1987), that the effects of imageability upon recall could be attributed to the enhanced distinctiveness of high-imagery items and the enhanced encoding of relationships amongst them. Although they were not entirely explicit about this in their article, Marschark et al. intended the same kind of explanation to apply to the effects of imagery mnemonic instructions (see Marschark & Cornoldi, 1991).

This account would predict that imagery instructions would have no effect (a) when subjects were prevented from encoding relational cues, or (b) when subjects were provided with some alternative basis for encoding relational information (as with thematically structured materials). The evidence discussed in the previous section concerning the effects of interactive and separative instructions constitutes extensive support for the first part of this prediction. Evidence for the second part comes from experiments on memory for complex ideas and memory for narrative prose.

I carried out an experiment based on a procedure which was originally devised by Bransford and Franks (1971), in which the subjects were tested on the retention of complex ideas and the particular sentences in which they were expressed (J.T.E. Richardson, 1985). For instance, the subjects were asked to remember the high-imagery sentences

- The jelly was sweet
- The ants in the kitchen ate the jelly
- The ants ate the sweet jelly which was on the table,

which defined a complex idea, "The ants in the kitchen ate the sweet jelly which was on the table." Similarly, the subjects were asked to remember the low-imagery sentences

- The attitude was arrogant
- The attitude led to immediate criticism
- The arrogant attitude expressed in the speech led to criticism,

which defined a complex idea, "The arrogant attitude expressed in the speech led to immediate criticism."

Three different groups of subjects were given standard instructions which did not specify any learning strategy, separative instructions which asked them to make up a single mental image for each sentence, and interactive instructions which asked them to make up complex images combining the events described by two or more sentences. There was no sign of any difference between the effects of interactive and separative instructions on any aspect of their performance, and there was no difference between these two groups and the subjects who had been given standard instructions in terms of their retention of the original ideas. Imagery instructions had no effect on the retention of high-imagery sentences, and they actually led to poorer retention of low-imagery sentences. I took this to mean that asking the subjects to make up images had simply imposed an irrelevant task which, being more demanding in the case of the low-imagery sentences, had interfered with their retention.

One study which is often cited as demonstrating beneficial effects of imagery instructions upon prose recall is the one by R.C. Anderson and Kulhavy (1972), which has already been mentioned in this chapter. It will be recalled that they compared the performance of subjects who were asked to form mental images with the performance of other subjects who were just asked to read a text. An initial analysis of the recall scores found no significant difference between the two groups, and this in itself might be taken to indicate that imagery instructions do not enhance prose learning. Anderson and Kulhavy also gave the subjects a post-test questionnaire in which they asked about the strategies used in the learning task. They found that the amount recalled was significantly related to the proportion of the passage for which the subjects reported that imagery had been employed, and they concluded that "a person will learn more from a prose passage if he forms images of the things and events described in the passage" (p. 243).

The results obtained by Anderson and Kulhavy are shown in Figure 5.1. Although there was indeed a significant effect of reported

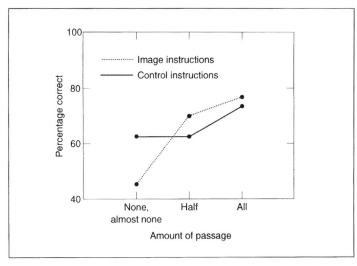

FIG. 5.1. Results of R.C. Anderson and Kulhavy (1972): percentage correct in the retention of narrative prose as a function of the amount of the passage for which the use of imagery was reported. From "Imagery and prose learning", by R.C. Anderson and R.W. Kulhavy, 1972, *Journal of Educational Psychology, 63,* 243. Copyright © 1972 by the American Psychological Association, Inc. Reprinted with permission.

use of imagery, this was qualified by a significant interaction with the effect of imagery instructions. If one inspects the results of the subjects who were given "control" instructions that did not mention a specific learning strategy, it is clear that there is very little variation in performance that could be related to the reported use of imagery. In fact, the significant overall effect of this variable is mainly due to the very poor performance of the subjects who reported that they had not used or tried to use imagery in order to carry out the learning task, despite the fact that they had been given explicit instructions to do so. This suggests that the beneficial relationship identified by Anderson and Kulhavy was actually spurious: as in my own study, the effects of imagery instructions, when they occur, appear to be primarily negative.

An exception to this pattern can be found in a series of experiments reported by Chaguiboff and Denis (1981) and Denis (1982), who tested subjects on their retention of information mentioned in narratives. The subjects were also classified as "high imagers" or "low imagers" according to their total scores on Marks's (1973) Vividness of Visual Imagery Questionnaire (VVIQ), which I discussed in Chapter 2. When the subjects were asked to read a simple narrative text at their own pace, high imagers remembered more of its content, but they also took longer to read the text than low imagers. One possibility, of course, is that high imagers simply tend to read more slowly and attentively and, as a result, remember more of what they have read. However, when a new group of subjects was asked to read a more abstract text taken from a psychology textbook, the high imagers and the low imagers did not differ in either their reading times or their subsequent retention. Moreover, in a further experiment, Denis asked subjects to read a narrative text as fast as possible. Under these circumstances, the difference between the reading times of the high imagers and the low imagers was not statistically significant, but the high imagers still remembered more than the low imagers. Indeed, there was hardly any difference in their retention scores compared with those obtained under self-paced conditions. This suggests that whatever the high imagers were doing during the extra time was not enhancing their retention of the text.

In a final experiment, Denis presented the narrative text to a new group of subjects under self-paced conditions, but this time they were asked to construct rich and vivid visual images of the places, characters, and actions described in the passage. Compared with the results obtained previously without any specific learning instructions, this led to a 19% increase in the reading times of the high imagers, but to a 40% increase in the times for low imagers, with the result that the two groups no longer differed significantly in terms of their overall reading times. Similarly, the imagery instructions increased the recognition scores obtained by the low imagers, but they did not significantly increase the scores obtained by the high imagers, with the result that the two groups no longer differed in their retention of the text, either.

At least in certain circumstances, then, imagery mnemonic instructions do enhance the retention of narrative prose. There is, however, a distinctive feature of the texts used in Denis' experiments, and this is that they tended to have a very strong spatial or geographic structure. In the experiment reported by Chaguiboff and Denis (1981), for instance, the text told the story of a trip by car, and it contained a series of passages describing various characters, scenes, and events that occurred along the way. In the experiments reported by Denis (1982), the text told the story of a farmer's wagon ride to a village to sell his crops and to go shopping, and of the various incidents that he encountered on his journey home. It is conceivable that the subjects in these experiments used imagery to make sense of the geographic information with which they were presented.

Indeed, as I mentioned in Chapter 2, subsequent research indicated that the images generated from verbal descriptions of maps were structurally similar to those based on the inspection of actual maps (Denis & Cocude, 1989, 1992, 1997). However, as I also pointed out in Chapter 2, scores on the VVIQ are usually only weakly related to performance on tests of learning and memory, if at all, and this conclusion extends to studies using discursive and narrative materials (see McKelvie, 1995). As a consequence, Denis' research must be regarded as an exception to a general pattern, albeit a very interesting one.

An analogous point can be made with regard to the studies reported by Cornoldi and De Beni (1991) and De Beni et al. (1997) that were mentioned earlier in this chapter. These researchers showed that use of the method of loci could enhance memory for narrative prose in comparison with the use of rote rehearsal. However, they had selected a control group of subjects who did not know about mnemonic devices and who therefore did not make spontaneous use of such devices. Moreover, they had evaluated recall performance primarily in terms of the subjects' ability to remember the order in which key ideas had appeared in the texts. This implies that the method of loci improves memory for serial order rather than memory for narrative prose *per se*.

Other research has failed to find any benefit from using the method of loci to remember texts. In fact, De Beni (1988) found that people who were instructed to use the method of loci performed less well than control subjects who were left to use their normal methods of studying texts. More generally, Perrig (1986) surveyed the published research on imagery instructions and prose learning, and found that in the majority of studies imagery instructions did not lead to a significant improvement in recall performance. This outcome is all the more remarkable, given that the publication policies of psychological journals are typically biased in favour of research papers which report statistically significant findings (see Mullen, 1989, p. 30).

Imagery instructions and brain function

In a study that I mentioned in Chapter 4, Goldenberg, Podreka, Steiner, and Willmes (1987) investigated patterns of regional cerebral blood flow whilst different subjects learned lists of high-imagery nouns either under standard instructions or under instructions to make up composite images relating together the words within each list. In a subsequent recognition test, the latter subjects achieved a much higher level of performance, confirming the effectiveness of the experimental instructions. The subjects who received standard instructions showed a slight rightward shift in the overall level of brain activation, but the subjects who received imagery instructions showed a slight leftward shift. The region of most pronounced asymmetry in the latter group was the left inferior occipital region, although these subjects also showed increased activation in both of the frontal lobes.

Most evidence on the neural mechanisms responsible for the beneficial effects of imagery instructions has come from the study of brain-damaged patients. Impaired memory function is a frequent outcome of brain damage; indeed, it is often itself a reliable sign that such damage has occurred. The fact that it is possible to enhance normal people's performance in learning and remembering by instructing them to use imagery suggests that a similar approach might be valuable in the treatment and rehabilitation of patients with brain dysfunction. This idea was first put forward by Patten (1972), who suggested that the classical mnemonic systems ''may be the foundation of a new branch of rehabilitation therapy helping patients to recover their memories'' (p. 26).

A number of investigations have shown that training and instructions in the use of mental imagery can enhance memory performance in patients with diffuse cerebral damage as the result of strokes, head injuries, or Parkinson's disease (see J.T.E. Richardson, 1995a). It will be remembered from Chapter 4 that in the case of head-injured patients I had found a selective impairment in their recall of high-imagery material such that they failed to show a significant advantage in the recall of high-imagery words in comparison to that of low-imagery words (J.T.E. Richardson, 1979b). However, in a subsequent study, we found that under imagery instructions both head-injured patients and orthopaedic controls produced better retention on high-imagery words than on low-imagery words, and there was no sign of any difference between the two groups in their level of retention (J.T.E. Richardson & Barry, 1985).

The results are shown in Table 5.1. Imagery instructions increased the head-injured patients' performance to the level demonstrated by the control subjects, and they reinstated the effect of imageability upon retention. We concluded that the effects of closed head injury upon memory should be attributed to the patients' failure to adopt the strategy of constructing interactive images. However, in Chapter 4, in accordance with the framework developed by Marschark et al. (1987), I suggested that this might reflect a more general problem with relational processing. On this view, head-injured patients do not engage in relational processing during the presentation of word lists

TABLE 5.1

| | Initial testing | | Final testing | |
	Concrete	Abstract	Concrete	Abstract
Standard instructions				
Orthopaedic controls	51.8	40.9	18.8	13.2
Head-injured patients	40.8	39.7	10.3	11.2
Imagery instructions				
Orthopaedic controls	56.6	48.8	22.3	10.2
Head-injured patients	54.5	47.5	20.5	9.1

Mean per cent correct in free recall for head-injured patients and for orthopaedic control subjects on concrete and abstract material in initial and final testing under standard learning instructions and imagery mnemonic instructions. From "The effects of minor closed head injury upon human memory: Further evidence on the role of mental imagery", by J.T.E. Richardson and C. Barry, 1985, *Cognitive Neuropsychology, 2*, 160. Copyright © 1985 by Lawrence Erlbaum Associates Ltd. Reprinted by permission of Psychology Press, UK.

unless they receive instructions specifically encouraging them to do so (for instance, by constructing interactive images).

Much of the early work on the potential therapeutic value of training in the use of imagery was carried out in patients with focal brain lesions, and was motivated by the hypothesis that the right hemisphere was somehow specialised for the use of mental imagery (see Chapter 1). This implied that a patient with brain damage restricted to the left hemisphere should be able to compensate for problems in verbal learning and memory by exploiting the preserved faculty of mental imagery within the intact right hemisphere. In accordance with this notion, Patten (1972) demonstrated that four patients with disorders of verbal memory attributed to focal lesions of the left cerebral hemisphere were able to use imagery mnemonics to improve their recall performance. Similar findings were obtained by M.K. Jones (1974) in the case of 18 epileptic patients who had undergone left temporal lobectomy, and by Gasparrini and Satz (1979) in the case of patients with verbal memory deficits caused by strokes involving the left hemisphere. In short, it is quite true that patients with left-hemisphere damage can benefit from training or instructions in the use of mental imagery.

However, the hypothesis of right-hemisphere specialisation for mental imagery also predicts that patients with focal brain lesions restricted to the right cerebral hemisphere should show a selective impairment in the use of mental imagery. The study by M.K. Jones (1974) included 18 other patients who had undergone surgical removal of the right temporal lobe, and Jones made the explicit prediction that these patients would derive less help from the use of an imagery mnemonic than normal subjects. In fact, these patients showed no sign of any impairment at all. In particular, they showed as much benefit as control subjects from instructions in the use of mental imagery.

Subsequent investigations of patients with unilateral lesions have confirmed that those with damage confined to the right hemisphere show the normal pattern of improved retention following the administration of imagery instructions (Shore, 1979; Vogel, Marko-witsch, Hempel, & Hackenberg, 1987). For instance, Goldenberg (1989) investigated recall performance on high-imagery paired associates under standard instructions and imagery instructions in patients with unilateral brain damage. As I mentioned in Chapter 4, the patients with lesions confined to the left hemisphere were profoundly impaired, but those with lesions confined to the right hemisphere were not. Both groups showed a relative improvement in performance following imagery instructions which was equivalent to the improvement shown by control subjects. When the performance of individual subjects was related to the anatomical site of their lesions according to computer tomography, it appeared that patients with lesions of the left occipito-temporal region had failed to benefit from imagery instructions in their recall of high-imagery pairs.

Nevertheless, the locus of brain damage in neurological patients typically depends upon the precise nature and cause of the brain damage. Relatively permanent, stable, and global impairments of memory can result from damage either to the temporal lobes or to the diencephalon, which is a region of the forebrain beneath the corpus callosum consisting primarily of the thalamus and the hypothalamus. In the former, impaired memory is mainly associated with bilateral temporal lobectomy, encephalitis due to the herpes simplex virus, and deficiency of oxygen in the brain tissues (anoxia), which can arise from a variety of causes. In the latter, impaired memory is mainly associated with Korsakoff's syndrome, thalamic infarction (i.e. strokes), and tumours of the third ventricle. A number of case studies have also suggested that similar (although often less severe) impairments can result from damage to areas within the frontal lobes (associated mainly with aneurysms of the anterior communicating artery) (see Parkin & Leng, 1993, Chapter 7).

Gade (1994) conducted a study to compare the effectiveness of imagery instructions in four groups of patients who were broadly similar in the severity of their memory impairment: 15 patients had undergone surgery for aneurysms of the anterior communicating artery; seven patients had diencephalic lesions associated with

Korsakoff's syndrome or a tumour of the third ventricle; six patients had bilateral temporal-lobe lesions associated with anoxia or encephalitis; and seven patients had brain damage from other causes. Gade found no significant difference among these four groups and concluded that the aetiology and hence the localisation of memory impairment was not a significant factor in the efficacy of mental imagery.

Gade then reclassified his amnesic patients into three groups in terms of the severity of their impairment as measured by their performance on a separate paired-associate learning task. This time, he found clear differences in the benefits gained from the administration of imagery instructions. The magnitude of the patients' improvement was inversely related to the severity of their memory impairment, and in particular the most severely amnesic patients showed little or no improvement at all as the result of instructions to generate mental images. In short, the primary clinical determinant of the effectiveness of mnemonic training in brain-damaged patients would seem to be the severity of the underlying memory deficit. Paradoxically, of course, this means that the benefits of imagery mnemonics will be inversely related to the patients' need for memory remediation (J.T.E. Richardson, 1995a).

Indeed, a number of studies have failed to find beneficial effects of imagery mnemonic instructions in severely amnesic patients. However, these patients seem to be perfectly capable of constructing mental images and are able to produce drawings that illustrate the interactive relationships contained within their images. When their task is highly structured and the memory load is minimal, such patients are sometimes able to benefit from the use of imagery as a mnemonic strategy. Even then, however, they may need to be prompted or reminded at the time of recall that they had originally used mental imagery to learn the critical material if they are to show any improvement in their performance.

For instance, M.K. Jones (1974) found that patients who had undergone bilateral temporal lobectomy appeared to forget that they had previously formed an imaginal association linking the items to be remembered and so were unable to use these images at the time of recall. Similarly, J.T.E. Richardson, Cermak, Blackford, and O'Connor (1987) described one patient with an aneurysm of the anterior communicating artery who had learned a variety of mnemonic aids prior to his disability. Despite being able to use these mnemonics in a spontaneous and appropriate manner, he remained densely amnesic. In conclusion, amnesic patients are able to form vivid and appropriate interactive images, but they do not appear to be able to use them to create effective memory representations without explicit mnemonic structure at the time of learning or without explicit prompting at the time of recall (J.T.E. Richardson, 1995a).

"Split-brain" patients are of particular interest in this connection. These patients have been shown to have impaired memory performance in some studies but not in others. It is not at present clear whether such effects are to be attributed to the actual surgical separation of the two hemispheres or to damage that may have occurred elsewhere in the brain (Parkin, 1984). However, Zaidel and Sperry (1974) suggested that human memory was normally facilitated by interactions between the cerebral hemispheres, and that the deficits shown by split-brain patients in verbal-learning tasks were attributable to the "lack of visual imagery support from the right hemisphere" (p. 270). In this context, the hypothesis of right-hemisphere specialisation of mental imagery implies that split-brain patients should show no benefit from training and instructions in the use of imagery mnemonics.

In possibly the earliest study of this nature, Gazzaniga, Risse, Springer, Clark, and Wilson (1975) tested four patients on the recall of two lists of paired associates. Three of the patients had undergone partial callosal sectioning, and hence some of the interhemispheric pathways were still intact. They showed a significant benefit when instructed to use imagery to learn the second list. The fourth patient, who had a complete commissurotomy, showed no such improvement. The fact that that partially sectioned patients were apparently able to encode the pairs into images, regardless of which pathways were preserved, was taken to mean that secondary forms of processed information "transfer readily across any available pathway" (p. 14). These results cannot be accepted at face value, however, because the performance of the completely sectioned patient was exceedingly poor throughout and thus subject to a floor effect; whereas the improved performance shown by the other three patients might have been merely the result of practice on an unfamiliar task.

In fact, several subsequent reports consistently appeared to show that patients who had undergone callosal section could exploit imagery to enhance their performance in verbal-learning tasks, which would entail that this can be achieved using only the mechanisms within the left or dominant cerebral hemisphere. Unfortunately, these were typically rather informal accounts in which the research methods and the results were insufficiently documented to allow any serious evaluation of the key findings. Fortunately, the crucial result was formally demonstrated by Milner, Taylor, and Jones-Gotman (1990). Their experiment was conducted with eight commissurotomy patients, of whom six were presumed to have undergone a complete surgical section of the interhemispheric commissures. As a group, the patients showed a significant improvement in the paired-associate learning of high-imagery words as a result of both experimenter-generated and self-generated imagery. This shows conclusively that the surgically isolated left cerebral hemisphere is fully capable of the use of imaginal encoding.

Summary: Imagery as a mnemonic strategy

1. The visualiser/verbaliser distinction was supposed to describe a predominant cognitive style. The habitual use of imagery predicts performance on spatial tests and the recall of pictures and of high-imagery words.
2. Imaginal and verbal strategies can be influenced by appropriate instructions, but they also depend on the demands of the task and the nature of the materials.
3. Subjects often report the use of imagery in learning paired associates consisting of high-imagery words, and this is associated with a high level of recall.
4. Interactive imagery instructions enhance recall but may be no more effective than verbal instructions; separative imagery instructions may have no effect; and imagery instructions may have no effect on memory for prose. Imagery instructions thus seem to improve performance by enhancing relational organisation.
5. The benefits of imagery mnemonics in patients with memory impairment following brain damage vary inversely with the severity of their memory impairment, but they seem to be largely unrelated to its precise aetiology.
6. Patients with damage restricted to the left hemisphere can often benefit from training in the use of mental imagery. However, the efficacy of imagery as a mnemonic strategy does not depend on the integrity of the right hemisphere. Indeed, mental imagery can provide an effective means of encoding verbal material even in split-brain patients.

7. The latter result indicates that imaginal encoding can be carried out using mechanisms within the left hemisphere. More specifically, evidence from brain imaging and from the study of patients with focal brain damage suggests that imaginal encoding depends on structures within the left occipito-temporal region.

Conclusions 6

I shall bring this book to a close by recapping some of the key points to have emerged from the previous chapters. I began the book by noting that cognitive psychologists had conceptualised imagery in different ways, and so I shall first review the main conclusions within each of these headings.

Imagery as a phenomenal experience

In Chapter 2, I pointed out that the phenomenal experience of imagery has to be investigated by collecting verbal accounts. These can be obtained by means of open-ended questions, which was the approach that was originally adopted by Galton (1880). This approach is used in research outside cognitive psychology into other forms of imaginal experience such as after-imagery, dreaming imagery, hallucinatory imagery, and hypnagogic imagery (the kind of experience that many people have on falling asleep and on waking up). Nevertheless, within cognitive psychology, it seems to be more useful to obtain quantitative ratings using instruments such as the Questionnaire upon Mental Imagery and the Vividness of Visual Imagery Questionnaire.

These instruments are generally satisfactory in terms of the standards on which psychometric tests are usually judged, and they are valuable for studying the qualitative aspects of personal experience (in particular, the vividness of imagery). Although reports of this sort are often not strongly related to people's objective performance on cognitive tasks, it could be argued that this is because they are not primarily intended for this purpose. Instruments such as the Individual Differences Questionnaire that measure the habitual use of imagery in the context of cognitively demanding situations do predict people's performance in tests of memory and spatial ability. People's reports on their actual use of imagery within particular tasks (such as solving spatial problems or paired-associate learning) can be excellent predictors of their objective performance.

Imagery as an internal representation

Indeed, images have certain functional properties that should enable them to be useful in a wide range of cognitive tasks, especially in spatial thinking and remembering. In Chapter 3, I described the role of imagery in tests of spatial ability. It would appear that imagined objects, events, and scenes are structurally equivalent to the physical objects, events, and scenes that they represent, and that they can be compared and manipulated in a manner that is analogous to the way in which real objects, events, and scenes are compared and manipulated.

The use of imagery as an internal representation appears to depend upon a system of visuo-spatial working memory which contains a passive store or visual buffer in which images can be constructed on the basis of information about the physical appearance of objects, events, and scenes that is held within long-term memory. I described two different theoretical views of this system, one developed by Baddeley and Hitch (1974) and more recently by Logie (1995), the other developed by Kosslyn (1980, 1994). Although there are certain differences between the two accounts, they are tending to converge upon a common understanding of the relationships between imagery and other aspects of human cognition.

Imagery as a stimulus attribute

In Chapter 4, I considered imagery as a property or attribute of the items that subjects have to deal with in psychological experiments. High-imagery items are better remembered than low-imagery items across a range of experimental tasks. This appears to be specifically related to the use of imagery as a visuo-spatial working memory, and it cannot be attributed to the purely linguistic properties of those items. Whilst the effect of item imageability within conventional experiments is probably one of the most robust findings in modern psychology, it is interesting that it sometimes does not arise with certain clinical populations, and this indicates that it may originate in a process that is under the subjects' strategic control.

The effect of imageability was originally regarded by some researchers as evidence for mental imagery as a separate code or representation in long-term memory (the assumption of "dual storage"). However, more recently it has been argued that it is equally consistent with the idea that the use of imagery is associated with different forms of relational and distinctive processing (the assumption of "dual processing"). Evidence for the dual-processing view and against the dual-storage view comes from recent demonstrations that effects of imageability can be abolished by preventing people from using encoded relations at the time of recall or by providing another basis for encoding relational information (such as thematic structure in the case of narrative prose).

Imagery as a mnemonic strategy

The idea that mental imagery can serve as an effective strategy for remembering new information has a very long history, but it is only relatively recently that it has been subjected to formal experimental investigation. The spontaneous use of imagery in verbal-learning tasks appears to be relatively high, according to questionnaires on people's habitual ways of thinking as well as reports of the mediators used in particular learning tasks. In both cases, the use of imagery is associated with relatively high levels of performance.

In addition, the use of imagery as a mnemonic strategy can be manipulated by giving appropriate training or instructions, although their effectiveness will also depend on the demands of the learning task and the nature of the material to be learned. The beneficial effect of imagery instructions in conventional experiments is another very robust finding within contemporary psychology, but once again this has to be qualified in certain interesting respects. The benefits depend specifically on the interactive nature of the images that are produced, and images appear to be no more effective than interactive verbal devices in supporting long-term memory. Finally, imagery instructions often do not improve the retention of narrative text. Imagery instructions, too, appear to improve performance by increasing relational processing rather than by involving a separate code or representation in long-term memory.

Imagery and the brain

One of the key principles underlying Kosslyn's (1980) account of imagery is that imagery should be regarded not as a unitary psychological function but as the product of a complex system of interrelating components or modules. If we now consider the question of the neuroanatomical underpinnings of imagery, this principle has one important implication: one should not assume that there is necessarily one single structure within the brain that is causally responsible for imagery; instead, the distinct components or modules may well be physically separated and thus distributed at different sites across the brain. This needs to be borne in mind in the following discussion.

However, it is still widely assumed that imagery is based upon a single mechanism in the brain, and that this mechanism is localised within the right cerebral hemisphere. Ehrlichman and Barrett (1983) provided an excellent critical analysis of this hypothesis and a comprehensive review of the evidence that was available. They came to the following conclusion:

> None of the studies, in our opinion, can be described as unequivocally supporting the hypothesis of right hemisphere specialization for mental imagery, and some appear to be inconsistent with such a formulation. (p. 72)

A good deal of evidence that is relevant to the hypothesis of a right-hemisphere specialisation for mental imagery has been produced since 1983. How, then, has Ehrlichman and Barrett's evaluation been affected by subsequent research?

First of all, verbal reports of the loss of imagery as a phenomenal experience tend to be associated with damage to the left hemisphere rather than to the right hemisphere. Research with physiological recording techniques has supported the idea of a left-hemisphere involvement in the experience of imagery. Second, the neural mechanisms responsible for generating images as mental representations also appear to be located within the left hemisphere, according to evidence from patients with brain damage and from physiological recording in people without brain damage. Finally, there is a limited amount of evidence to link the effectiveness of imagery as a mnemonic strategy with areas within the left hemisphere.

There is in fact little evidence, if any, that damage to the right hemisphere can disrupt the phenomenal experience of imagery or the patients' ability to use imagery as a mnemonic strategy. The right hemisphere appears to be involved in the transformation and manipulation of images once they have been generated by structures within the left hemisphere, and hence damage to the right hemisphere can give rise to impairment on tasks that require spatial visualisation. It also appears to be implicated in the relational processing underlying effects of imageability, insofar as these effects persist in patients with damage to the left hemisphere, and also insofar as these effects are associated with activation of both hemispheres in intact subjects.

Important evidence on many of these points has come from the study of split-brain patients. Although such patients may have memory impairments and other cognitive problems, they are able to report their experience of imagery, both in dreams and in waking life, and they can use imagery as a mediating device in verbal-learning tasks. At least some split-brain patients are able to generate mental images but appear to have problems in mental rotation and other transformations.

I do need to acknowledge that other reviewers consider the research evidence on this topic not to be entirely consistent (see, for example, Farah, 1989). Sergent (1990) suggested that the most reasonable conclusion was that both hemispheres could contribute simultaneously and conjointly to the process of image generation. Nevertheless, as Tippett (1992) pointed out, until recently imagery was considered to be so obviously a faculty of the right hemisphere that the question was seldom explicitly discussed. Consequently, the idea that the left hemisphere is involved in image generation at all represents a shift of some magnitude in psychological thinking.

Moreover, within the left hemisphere, there are consistent suggestions that an area in the posterior portion of the brain, possibly in the inferior occipital or occipito-parietal region, is particularly important in the mechanism of image generation. These are currently still somewhat speculative suggestions, but they have come from experiments both on spatial visualisation and on the effectiveness of imagery instructions, and they are based both upon the study of brain-damaged patients and upon physiological recording in normal individuals. Kosslyn (1994) inferred that the mechanisms involved in mental imagery may be intimately related to the mechanisms responsible for perceptual analysis and linguistic comprehension in the left hemisphere. However, the primary visual cortex does not seem to be involved in either the function or the experience of visual imagery.

In Chapter 3, I mentioned an article by J.R. Anderson (1978), who offered a formal proof of the proposition that the behavioural output of a theory based upon mental imagery could always be reproduced by another theory that made no reference to imagery at all. At the time, many psychologists, especially in North America, felt that this argument left imagery research in a stalemate. Indeed, at a conference in the mid-1980s, an eminent American psychologist suggested to me that Anderson's article had killed off imagery research altogether.

I hope that in this book I have shown that reports of the death of imagery research are certainly exaggerated. This is a very lively field to which researchers around the world (though especially within Europe) are currently contributing, and it is continuing to provide cognitive psychology with new ideas, new theories, new insights, and new discoveries. More than that, however, by linking the study of the mind to the study of the brain, imagery research has provided a very effective riposte to Anderson's attack. As Kosslyn (1994) commented:

> When behavioral data alone are not sufficient to resolve an issue, the tasks designed by experimental psychologists can be used to selectively activate specific brain systems while neural activity is being monitored and to study the consequences of brain damage—and these additional data can settle many issues. (p. 407)

This is a very powerful message for cognitive psychologists, which will, among other things, ensure that imagery remains a focus for their investigations for the foreseeable future.

Summary: Conclusions

1. The different ways of conceptualising mental imagery have each given rise to important findings concerning the involvement of imagery in human cognition.
2. Structures within the posterior portion of the left hemisphere of the brain appear to be crucial to the generation and the experience of imagery. Structures in the right hemisphere appear to be involved in the transformation and the manipulation of mental images.
3. Imagery research is an example to cognitive psychologists of how fundamental conceptual, theoretical, and empirical questions concerning human cognition can be addressed by linking the study of the mind to the study of the brain.

References

Albert, M.L. (1973). A simple test of visual neglect. *Neurology, 23*, 658–664.

Alesandrini, K.L. (1981). Pictorial–verbal and analytic–holistic learning strategies in science learning. *Journal of Educational Psychology, 73*, 358–368.

Anderson, B. (1993). Spared awareness for the left side of internal visual images in patients with left-sided extrapersonal neglect. *Neurology, 43*, 213–216.

Anderson, J.R. (1978). Arguments concerning representations for mental imagery. *Psychological Review, 85*, 249–277.

Anderson, J.R., & Bower, G.H. (1973). *Human associative memory.* Washington, DC: Winston.

Anderson, R.C., & Kulhavy, R.W. (1972). Imagery and prose learning. *Journal of Educational Psychology, 63*, 242–243.

Ashton, R., & White, K.D. (1980). Sex differences in imagery vividness: An artifact of the test. *British Journal of Psychology, 71*, 35–38.

Baddeley, A.D. (1986). *Working memory.* Oxford: Oxford University Press.

Baddeley, A., & Andrade, J. (1998). Working memory and consciousness: An empirical approach. In M.A. Conway, S.E. Gathercole, & C. Cornoldi (Eds), *Theories of memory II* (pp. 1–24). Hove, UK: Psychology Press.

Baddeley, A.D., Grant, S., Wight, E., & Thomson, N. (1975). Imagery and visual working memory. In P.M.A. Rabbitt & S. Dornic (Eds), *Attention and performance V* (pp. 205–217). London: Academic Press.

Baddeley, A.D., & Hitch, G. (1974). Working memory. In G. H. Bower (Ed.), *The psychology of learning and motivation: Advances in research and theory* (Vol. 8, pp. 47–89). New York: Academic Press.

Baddeley, A.D., & Lieberman, K. (1980). Spatial working memory. In R.S. Nickerson (Ed.), *Attention and performance VIII* (pp. 521–539). Hillsdale, NJ: Erlbaum.

Baddeley, A.D., Thomson, N., & Buchanan, M. (1975). Word length and the structure of short-term memory. *Journal of Verbal Learning and Verbal Behavior, 14*, 575–589.

Bakan, P. (1969). Hypnotizability, laterality of eye-movements and functional brain asymmetry. *Perceptual and Motor Skills, 28*, 927–932.

Bakan, P., & Strayer, F.F. (1973). On reliability of conjugate lateral eye movements. *Perceptual and Motor Skills, 36*, 429–430.

Barbut, D., & Gazzaniga, M.S. (1987). Disturbances in conceptual space involving language and speech. *Brain, 110*, 1487–1496.

Barratt, P.E. (1953). Imagery and thinking. *Australian Journal of Psychology, 5*, 154–164.

Bartlett, F.C. (1932). *Remembering: A study in experimental and social psychology.* London: Cambridge University Press.

Bartolomeo, P., D'Erme, P., & Gainotti, G. (1994). The relationship between visuo-spatial and representational neglect. *Neurology, 44*, 1710–1714.

Basso, A., Bisiach, E., & Luzzatti, C. (1980). Loss of mental imagery: A case study. *Neuropsychologia, 18*, 435–442.

Beatty, W.W., & Butters, N. (1986). Further analysis of encoding in patients with Huntington's disease. *Brain and Cognition, 5*, 387–398.

Begg, I. (1972). Recall of meaningful phrases. *Journal of Verbal Learning and Verbal Behavior, 11*, 431–439.

Begg, I. (1978). Imagery and organization in memory: Instructional effects. *Memory and Cognition, 6*, 174–183.

Benjafield, J., & Muckenheim, R. (1989). Dates of entry and measures of imagery, concreteness, goodness, and familiarity for 1,046 words sampled from the *Oxford English Dictionary. Behavior Research Methods, Instruments, and Computers, 21*, 31–52.

Berg, M.R., & Harris, L.J. (1980). The effect of experimenter location and subject anxiety on cerebral activation as measured by lateral eye movements. *Neuropsychologia, 18*, 89–93.

Berger, G.H., & Gaunitz, S.C.B. (1977). Self–rated imagery and vividness of task pictures in relation to visual memory. *British Journal of Psychology, 68*, 283–288.

Berlyne, D.E. (1965). *Structure and direction in thinking.* New York: Wiley.

Beschin, N., Cocchini, G., Della Sala, S., & Logie, R.H. (1997). What the eyes perceive, the brain ignores: A case of pure unilateral representational neglect. *Cortex, 33*, 3–26.

Betts, G.H. (1909). *The distribution and functions of mental imagery* (Contributions to Education, No. 26). New York: Columbia University, Teachers College.

Bisiach, E., Capitani, E., Luzzatti, C., & Perani, D. (1981). Brain and conscious representation of outside reality. *Neuropsychologia, 19*, 543–551.

Bisiach, E., & Luzzatti, C. (1978). Unilateral neglect of representational space. *Cortex, 14*, 129–133.

Bisiach, E., Luzzatti, C., & Perani, D. (1979). Unilateral neglect, representational scheme and consciousness. *Brain, 102*, 609–618.

Bobrow, S.A., & Bower, G.H. (1969). Comprehension and recall of sentences. *Journal of Experimental Psychology, 80*, 455–461.

Bonin, G. von, & Bailey, P. (1947). *Neocortex of Macaca mulatta.* Urbana, IL: University of Illinois Press.

Bower, G.H. (1970). Imagery as a relational organizer in associative learning. *Journal of Verbal Learning and Verbal Behavior, 9*, 539–533.

Bower, G.H. (1972). Mental imagery and associative learning. In L.W. Gregg (Ed.), *Cognition in learning and memory* (pp. 51–88). New York: Wiley.

Brandimonte, M.A., & Gerbino, W. (1993). Mental image reversal and verbal recoding: When ducks become rabbits. *Memory and Cognition, 21*, 23–33.

Bransford, J.D., & Franks, J.J. (1971). The abstraction of linguistic ideas. *Cognitive Psychology, 2*, 331–350.

Brener, R. (1940). An experimental investigation of memory span. *Journal of Experimental Psychology, 26*, 467–482.

Brooks, L.R. (1967). The suppression of visualization by reading. *Quarterly Journal of Experimental Psychology, 19*, 289–299.

Bruyer, R., & Racquez, F. (1985). Are lateral differences in word processing modulated by concreteness, imageability, both, or neither? *International Journal of Neuroscience, 27*, 181–189.

Buschke, H. (1973). Selective reminding for analysis of memory and learning. *Journal of Verbal Learning and Verbal Behavior, 12*, 543–550.

Byrne, B. (1974). Item concreteness vs spatial organization as predictors of visual imagery. *Memory and Cognition, 2*, 53–59.

Cantor, D.S., Andreassen, C., & Waters, H.S. (1985). Organization in visual episodic memory: Relationships between verbalized knowledge, strategy use, and performance. *Journal of Experimental Child Psychology, 40*, 218–232.

Chaguiboff, J., & Denis, M. (1981). Activité d'imagerie et reconnaissance de noms provenant d'un texte narratif. *L'Année Psychologique, 81*, 69–86.

Chambers, D., & Reisberg, D. (1985). Can mental images be ambiguous? *Journal of Experimental Psychology: Human Perception and Performance, 11*, 317–328.

Cohen, B.H., & Saslona, M. (1990). The advantage of being an habitual visualizer. *Journal of Mental Imagery, 14*(3 & 4), 101–112.

Cohen, M.S., Kosslyn, S.M., Breiter, H.C., DiGirolamo, G.J., Thompson, W.L., Anderson, A.K., Bookheimer, S.Y., Rosen, B.R., & Belliveau, J.W. (1996). Changes in cortical activity during mental rotation: A mapping study using functional MRI. *Brain, 119*, 89–100.

Cohen, W., & Polich, J. (1989). No hemispheric differences for mental rotation of letters or polygons. *Bulletin of the Psychonomic Society, 27*, 25–28.

Coltheart, M. (1980). Deep dyslexia: A right–hemisphere hypothesis. In M. Coltheart, K. Patterson, & J.C. Marshall (Eds), *Deep dyslexia* (pp. 326–380). London: Routledge & Kegan Paul.

Cooper, L.A., & Shepard, R.N. (1973). Chronometric studies of the rotation of mental images. In W.G. Chase (Ed.), *Visual information processing* (pp. 75–176). New York: Academic Press.

Corballis, M.C. (1982). Mental rotation: Anatomy of a paradigm. In M. Potegal (Ed.), *Spatial abilities: Developmental and physiological foundations* (pp. 173–198). New York: Academic Press.

Corballis, M.C., & Sergent, J. (1988). Imagery in a commissurotomized patient. *Neuropsychologia, 26*, 13–26.

Corballis, M.C., & Sergent, J. (1989). Mental rotation in a commissurotomized patient. *Neuropsychologia, 27*, 585–598.

Cornoldi, C., & De Beni, R. (1991). Memory for discourse: Loci mnemonics and the oral presentation effect. *Applied Cognitive Psychology, 5*, 511–518.

Cornoldi, C., Logie, R., Brandimonte, M., Kaufmann, G., & Reisberg, D. (1996). *Stretching the imagination: Representation and transformation in mental imagery*. New York: Oxford University Press.

Davidson, R.J., & Schwartz, G.E. (1977). Brain mechanisms subserving self-generated imagery: Electrophysiological specificity and patterning. *Psychophysiology, 14*, 598–601.

De Beni, R. (1988). The aid given by the "loci" memory technique in the memorization of passages. In M.M. Gruneberg, P.E. Morris, & R.N. Sykes (Eds), *Practical aspects of memory: Current research and issues: Vol. 2. Clinical and Educational Implications* (pp. 421–424). Chichester, UK: Wiley.

De Beni, R., Moè, A., & Cornoldi, C. (1997). Learning from texts or lectures: Loci mnemonics can interfere with reading but not with listening. *European Journal of Cognitive Psychology, 9*, 401–415.

Decety, J. (1996). Do imagined and executed actions share the same neural substrate? *Cognitive Brain Research, 3*, 87–93.

Decety, J., & Ingvar, D.H. (1990). Brain structures participating in mental simulation of motor behavior: A neuropsychological interpretation. *Acta Psychologica, 73*, 13–34.

Denis, M. (1982). Imaging while reading text: A study of individual differences. *Memory and Cognition, 10*, 540–545.

Denis, M., & Cocude, M. (1989). Scanning visual images generated from verbal descriptions. *European Journal of Cognitive Psychology, 1*, 293–307.

Denis, M., & Cocude, M. (1992). Structural properties of visual images constructed from poorly or well-structured verbal descriptions. *Memory and Cognition, 20*, 497–506.

Denis, M., & Cocude, M. (1997). On the metric properties of visual images generated from verbal descriptions: Evidence for the robustness of the mental scanning effect. *European Journal of Cognitive Psychology, 9*, 353–379.

De Renzi, E., & Nichelli, P. (1975). Verbal and non-verbal short-term memory impairment following hemispheric damage. *Cortex, 11*, 341–354.

D'Esposito, M., Detre, J.A., Aguirre, G.K., Stallcup, M., Alsop, D.C., Tippet, L.J., & Farah, M.J. (1997). A functional MRI study of mental image generation. *Neuropsychologia, 35*, 725–730.

Deutsch, G., Bourbon, T., Papanicolaou, A.C., & Eisenberg, H.M. (1988). Visuospatial tasks compared via activation of regional cerebral blood flow. *Neuropsychologia, 26*, 445–452.

Di Vesta, F.J., & Sunshine, P.M. (1974). The retrieval of abstract and concrete materials as functions of imagery, mediation, and mnemonic aids. *Memory and Cognition, 2*, 340–344.

Drachman, D.A., & Sahakian, B.J. (1979). Effects of cholinergic agents on human learning and memory. In A. Barbeau, J.H. Growdon, & R.J. Wurtman (Eds), *Nutrition and the brain: Vol. 5. Choline and lecithin in brain disorders* (pp. 351–366). New York: Raven Press.

Edwards, J.E., & Wilkins, W. (1981). Verbalizer–Visualizer Questionnaire: Relationship with imagery and verbal–visual ability. *Journal of Mental Imagery, 5*(2), 137–142.

Ehrlichman, H., & Barrett, J. (1983). Right hemispheric specialization for mental imagery: A review of the evidence. *Brain and Cognition, 2*, 55–76.

Ehrlichman, H., & Weinberger, A. (1978). Lateral eye movements and hemispheric asymmetry: A critical review. *Psychological Bulletin, 85*, 1080–1101.

Einstein, G.O., & McDaniel, M.A. (1987). Distinctiveness and the mnemonic effects of bizarre imagery. In M.A. McDaniel & M. Pressley (Eds), *Imagery and related mnemonic processes: Theories, individual differences, and applications* (pp. 78–102). New York: Springer-Verlag.

Ericsson, K.A., & Simon, H.A. (1993). *Protocol analysis: Verbal reports as data* (rev. ed.). Cambridge, MA: MIT Press.

Ernest, C.H. (1983). Imagery and verbal ability and recognition memory for pictures and words in males and females. *Educational Psychology, 3*, 227–244.

Fancher, R.W. (1994). Historical background of psychology. In A.M. Colman (Ed.), *Companion encyclopedia of psychology* (Vol. 1, pp. 19–37). London: Routledge.

Farah, M.J. (1984). The neurological basis of mental imagery: A componential analysis. *Cognition, 18*, 245–272.

Farah, M.J. (1988). Is visual imagery really visual? Overlooked evidence from neuropsychology. *Psychological Review, 95*, 307–317.

Farah, M.J. (1989). The neuropsychology of mental imagery. In F. Boller & J. Grafman (Eds), *Handbook of neuropsy-*

chology (Vol. 2, pp. 395–413). Amsterdam: Elsevier.

Farah, M.J., Gazzaniga, M.S., Holtzman, J.D., & Kosslyn, S.M. (1985). A left hemisphere basis for visual mental imagery? *Neuropsychologia, 23,* 115–118.

Farah, M.J., Hammond, K.M., Levine, D.N., & Calvanio, R. (1988). Visual and spatial mental imagery: Dissociable systems of representation. *Cognitive Psychology, 20,* 439–462.

Farah, M.J., Levine, D.N., & Calvanio, R. (1988). A case study of mental imagery deficit. *Brain and Cognition, 8,* 147–164.

Finke, R.A. (1989). *Principles of mental imagery.* Cambridge, MA: MIT Press.

Friedland, R.P., & Weinstein, E.A. (1977). Hemi-inattention and hemisphere specialization: Introduction and historical review. In E.A. Weinstein & R.P. Friedland (Eds), *Hemi-inattention and hemisphere specialization (Advances in Neurology,* Vol. 18, pp. 1–31). New York: Raven Press.

Friedman, A. (1978). Memorial comparisons without the "mind's eye". *Journal of Verbal Learning and Verbal Behavior, 17,* 427–444.

Friendly, M., Franklin, P.E., Hoffman, D., & Rubin, D.C. (1982). The Toronto Word Pool: Norms for imagery, concreteness, orthographic variables, and grammatical usage for 1,080 words. *Behavior Research Methods and Instrumentation, 14,* 375–399.

Frith, C.D., Richardson, J.T.E., Samuel, M., Crow, T.J., & McKenna, P.J. (1984). The effects of intravenous diazepam and hyoscine upon human memory. *Quarterly Journal of Experimental Psychology, 36A,* 133–144.

Gade, A. (1994). Imagery as a mnemonic aid in amnesia patients: Effects of amnesia subtype and severity. In M.J. Riddoch & G.W. Humphreys (Eds), *Cognitive neuropsychology and cognitive*

rehabilitation (pp. 571–589). Hove, UK: Laurence Erlbaum Associates Ltd.

Galton, F. (1880). Statistics of mental imagery. *Mind, 5,* 301–318.

Galton, F. (1883). *Inquiries into human faculty and its development.* London: Macmillan.

Gasparrini, B., & Satz, P. (1979). A treatment for memory problems in left hemisphere CVA patients. *Journal of Clinical Neuropsychology, 1,* 137–150.

Gazzaniga, M.S., & LeDoux, J.E. (1978). *The integrated mind.* New York: Plenum Press.

Gazzaniga, M.S., Risse, G.L., Springer, S.P., Clark, E., & Wilson, D.H. (1975). Psychologic and neurologic consequences of partial and complete cerebral commissurotomy. *Neurology, 25,* 10–15.

Gloor, P., Olivier, A., Quesney, L.F., Andermann, F., & Horowitz, S. (1982). The role of the limbic system in experiential phenomena of temporal lobe epilepsy. *Annals of Neurology, 12,* 129–144.

Goldenberg, G. (1989). The ability of patients with brain damage to generate mental visual images. *Brain, 112,* 305–325.

Goldenberg, G., Podreka, I., & Steiner, M. (1990). The cerebral localization of visual imagery: Evidence from emission computerized tomography of cerebral blood flow. In P.J. Hampson, D.F. Marks, & J.T.E. Richardson (Eds), *Imagery: Current developments* (pp. 307–332). London: Routledge.

Goldenberg, G., Podreka, I., Steiner, M., Suess, E., Deecke, L., & Willmes, K. (1988). Pattern of regional cerebral blood flow related to visual and motor imagery: Results of emission computerized tomography. In M. Denis, J. Engelkamp, & J.T.E. Richardson (Eds), *Cognitive and neuropsychological* approaches to mental imagery (pp. 363–373). Dordrecht: Martinus Nijhoff.

Goldenberg, G., Podreka, I., Steiner, M., & Willmes, K. (1987). Patterns of regional cerebral blood flow related to meaningfulness and imaginability of words: An emission computer tomography study. Neuropsychologia, 25, 473–485.

Gordon, R. (1949). An investigation into some of the factors that favour the formation of stereotyped images. British Journal of Psychology, 39, 156–167.

Green, K.E., & Schroeder, D.H. (1990). Psychometric quality of the Verbalizer–Visualizer Questionnaire as a measure of cognitive style. Psychological Reports, 66, 939–945.

Grossi, D., Modafferi, A., Pelosi, L., & Trojano, L. (1989). On the different roles of the cerebral hemisphere in mental imagery: The "o'clock test" in two clinical cases. Brain and Cognition, 10, 18–27.

Guariglia, C., Padovani, A., Pantano, P., & Pizzamiglio, L. (1993). Unilateral neglect restricted to visual imagery. Nature, 364, 235–237.

Guilford, J.P., Fruchter, B., & Zimmerman, W.S. (1952). Factor analysis of the Army Air Forces Sheppard Field battery of experimental aptitude tests. Psychometrika, 17, 45–68.

Gur, R.C., & Hilgard, E.R. (1975). Visual imagery and the discrimination of differences between altered pictures simultaneously and successively presented. British Journal of Psychology, 66, 341–345.

Halgren, E., Walter, R.D., Cherlow, D.G., & Crandall, P.H. (1978). Mental phenomena evoked by electrical stimulation of the human hippocampal formation and amygdala. Brain, 101, 83–117.

Halligan, P.W., & Marshall, J.C. (1992). Left visuo-spatial neglect: A meaningless entity? Cortex, 28, 525–535.

Harris, L.J. (1978). Sex differences in spatial ability: Possible environmental, genetic, and neurological factors. In M. Kinsbourne (Ed.), Asymmetrical function of the brain (pp. 405–522). Cambridge, UK: Cambridge University Press.

Harshman, R.A., & Paivio, A. (1987). "Paradoxical" sex differences in self-reported imagery. Canadian Journal of Psychology, 41, 287–302.

Haynes, W.O., & Moore, W.H. (1981). Sentence memory and recall: An electroencephalographic evaluation of hemispheric processing in males and females. Cortex, 17, 49–62.

Hiscock, M. (1976). Effects of adjective imagery on recall from prose. Journal of General Psychology, 94, 295–299.

Hiscock, M. (1978). Imagery assessment through self-report: What do imagery questionnaires measure? Journal of Consulting and Clinical Psychology, 46, 223–230.

Hoc, J.M., & Leplat, J. (1983). Evaluation of different modalities of verbalization in a sorting task. International Journal of Man–Machine Studies, 18, 283–306.

Holt, R.R. (1964). Imagery: The return of the ostracized. American Psychologist, 19, 254–264.

Hyman, I.E., Jr. (1993). Imagery, reconstructive memory, and discovery. In B. Roskos–Ewoldson, M.J. Intons-Peterson, & R.E. Anderson (Eds), Imagery, creativity, and discovery: A cognitive perspective (pp. 99–121). Amsterdam: Elsevier.

Indow, T., & Togano, K. (1970). On retrieving sequence from long–term memory. Psychological Review, 77, 317–331.

Intons-Peterson, M.J. (1983). Imagery paradigms: How vulnerable are they to experimenters' expectations? Journal of Experimental Psychology: Human Perception and Performance, 9, 394–412.

Isaac, A.R., & Marks, D.F. (1994). Individual differences in mental imagery experience: Developmental changes and specialization. *British Journal of Psychology, 85,* 479–500.

Isaac, A., Marks, D.F., & Russell, D.G. (1986). An instrument for assessing imagery of movement: The Vividness of Movement Imagery Questionnaire. *Journal of Mental Imagery, 10*(4), 23–30.

Janssen, W.H. (1976a). Selective interference during the retrieval of visual images. *Quarterly Journal of Experimental Psychology, 28,* 535–539.

Janssen, W.H. (1976b). Selective interference in paired-associate and free recall learning: Messing up the image. *Acta Psychologica, 40,* 35–48.

Jones, G.V. (1988). Images, predicates, and retrieval cues. In M. Denis, J. Engelkamp, & J.T.E. Richardson (Eds), *Cognitive and neuropsychological approaches to mental imagery* (pp. 89–98). Dordrecht: Martinus Nijhoff.

Jones, M.K. (1974). Imagery as a mnemonic aid after left temporal lobectomy: Contrast between material-specific and generalized memory disorders. *Neuropsychologia, 12,* 21–30.

Jones-Gotman, M. (1979). Incidental learning of image-mediated or pronounced words after right temporal lobectomy. *Cortex, 15,* 187–197.

Kapur, N. (1988). *Memory disorders in clinical practice.* London: Butterworths.

Kaufmann, G., & Helstrup, T. (1993). Mental imagery: Fixed or multiple meanings? Nature and function of imagery in creative thinking. In B. Roskos-Ewoldson, M.J. Intons-Peterson, & R.E. Anderson (Eds), *Imagery, creativity, and discovery: A cognitive perspective* (pp. 123–150). Amsterdam: Elsevier.

Kinsbourne, M. (1972). Eye and head turning indicates cerebral lateralization. *Science, 176,* 539–541.

Kintsch, W. (1972). Abstract nouns: Imagery versus lexical complexity. *Journal of Verbal Learning and Verbal Behavior, 11,* 59–65.

Kirby, J.R., Moore, P.J., & Schofield, N.J. (1988). Verbal and visual learning styles. *Contemporary Educational Psychology, 13,* 169–184.

Kocel, K., Galin, D., Ornstein, R., & Merrin, E.L. (1972). Lateral eye movement and cognitive mode. *Psychonomic Science, 27,* 223–224.

Kopelman, M.D. (1986). The cholinergic neurotransmitter system in human memory and dementia: A review. *Quarterly Journal of Experimental Psychology, 38A,* 535–573.

Kosslyn, S.M. (1973). Scanning visual images: Some structural implications. *Perception and Psychophysics, 14,* 90–94.

Kosslyn, S.M. (1980). *Image and mind.* Cambridge, MA: Harvard University Press.

Kosslyn, S.M. (1987). Seeing and imagining in the cerebral hemispheres: A computational approach. *Psychological Review, 94,* 148–175.

Kosslyn, S.M. (1994). *Image and brain: The resolution of the imagery debate.* Cambridge, MA: MIT Press.

Kosslyn, S.M., Alpert, N.M., Thompson, W.L., Maljkovic, V., Weise, S.B., Chabris, C.F., Hamilton, S.E., Rauch, S.L., & Buonanno, F.S. (1993). Visual mental imagery activates topographically organized visual cortex: PET investigations. *Journal of Cognitive Neuroscience, 5,* 263–287.

Kosslyn, S.M., Brunn, J., Cave, K.R., & Wallach, R.W. (1984). Individual differences in mental imagery ability: A computational analysis. *Cognition, 18,* 195–243.

Kosslyn, S.M., Holtzman, J.D., Farah, M.J., & Gazzaniga, M.S. (1985). A computational analysis of mental image generation: Evidence from functional dissociations in split-brain patients. *Journal of Experimental Psychology: General*, 114, 311–341.

Kosslyn, S.M., & Koenig, O. (1992). *Wet mind: The new cognitive neuroscience.* New York: Free Press.

Kosslyn, S.M., & Pomerantz, J.R. (1977). Imagery, propositions, and the form of internal representation. *Cognitive Psychology*, 9, 52–76.

Kosslyn, S.M., Van Kleeck, M.H., & Kirby, K.N. (1990). A neurologically plausible model of individual differences in visual mental imagery. In P.J. Hampson, D.F. Marks, & J.T.E. Richardson (Eds), *Imagery: Current developments* (pp. 39–77). London: Routledge.

Lambert, A.J., & Beaumont, J.G. (1981). Comparative processing of imageable nouns in the left and right visual fields. *Cortex*, 17, 411–418.

Levin, H.S., & Goldstein, F.C. (1986). Organization of verbal memory after severe closed-head injury. *Journal of Clinical and Experimental Neuropsychology*, 8, 643–656.

Levine, D.N., Warach, J., & Farah, M. (1985). Two visual systems in mental imagery: Dissociation of "what" and "where" in imagery disorders due to bilateral posterior cerebral lesions. *Neurology*, 35, 1010–1018.

Ley, R.G. (1983). Cerebral laterality and imagery. In A.A. Sheikh (Ed.), *Imagery: Current theory, research and application* (pp. 252–287). New York: Wiley.

Linn, M.C., & Petersen, A.C. (1985). Emergence and characterization of sex differences in spatial ability: A meta-analysis. *Child Development*, 56, 1479–1498.

Lister, R.G., & Weingartner, H.J. (1987). Neuropharmacological strategies for understanding psychobiological determinants of cognition. *Human Neurobiology*, 6, 119–127.

Loftus, E.F., & Loftus, G.R. (1980). On the permanence of stored information in the human brain. *American Psychologist*, 35, 409–420.

Logie, R.H. (1986). Visuo-spatial processes in working memory. *Quarterly Journal of Experimental Psychology*, 38A, 229–247.

Logie, R.H. (1995). *Visuo-spatial working memory.* Hove, UK: Lawrence Erlbaum Associates Ltd.

Logie, R.H. (1996). The seven ages of working memory. In J.T.E. Richardson, R.W. Engle, L. Hasher, R.H. Logie, E.R. Stoltzfus, & R.T. Zacks, *Working memory and human cognition* (pp. 31–65). New York: Oxford University Press.

Lorenz, C., & Neisser, U. (1985). Factors of imagery and event recall. *Memory and Cognition*, 13, 494–500.

McDaniel, M.A., & Kearney, E.M. (1984). Optimal learning strategies and their spontaneous use: The importance of task-appropriate processing. *Memory and Cognition*, 12, 361–373.

McDaniel, M.A., & Pressley, M. (1984). Putting the keyword method in context. *Journal of Educational Psychology*, 76, 598–609.

McDougall, S., & Velmans, M. (1993). Encoding strategy dynamics: When relationships between words determine strategy use. *British Journal of Psychology*, 84, 227–248.

McGeer, P.L. (1984). Aging, Alzheimer's disease, and the cholinergic system. *Canadian Journal of Physiology and Pharmacology*, 62, 741–754.

McKelvie, S.J. (1979). Effects of instruction and format on reported visual imagery. *Perceptual and Motor Skills*, 49, 567–571.

McKelvie, S.J. (1986). Effects of format of the Vividness of Visual Imagery Questionnaire on content validity, split-half reliability, and the role of memory in test–retest reliability. *British Journal of Psychology, 77,* 229–236.

McKelvie, S.J. (1995). The VVIQ as a psychometric test of individual differences in visual imagery vividness: A critical quantitative review and plea for direction. *Journal of Mental Imagery, 19*(3 & 4), 1–106.

Mandler, G. (1967). Organization and memory. In K.W. Spence & J.T. Spence (Eds), *The psychology of learning and motivation: Advances in research and theory* (Vol. 1, pp. 327–372). New York: Academic Press.

Marks, D.F. (1973). Visual imagery differences in the recall of pictures. *British Journal of Psychology, 64,* 17–24.

Marks, D.F. (1983). Mental imagery and consciousness: A theoretical review. In A.A. Sheikh (Ed.), *Imagery: Current theory, research, and application* (pp. 96–130). New York: Wiley.

Marks, D.F. (1990). On the relationship between imagery, body and mind. In P.J. Hampson, D.F. Marks, & J.T.E. Richardson (Eds), *Imagery: Current developments* (pp. 1–38). London: Routledge.

Marks, D.F., & Isaac, A.R. (1995). Topographical distribution of EEG activity accompanying visual and motor imagery in vivid and non-vivid imagers. *British Journal of Psychology, 86,* 271–282.

Marquer, J., & Pereira, M. (1990). Reaction times in the study of strategies in sentence–picture verification: A reconsideration. *Quarterly Journal of Experimental Psychology, 42A,* 147–168.

Marschark, M. (1985). Imagery and organization in the recall of prose. *Journal of Memory and Language, 24,* 734–745.

Marschark, M., & Cornoldi, C. (1991). Imagery and verbal memory. In C. Cornoldi & M.A. McDaniel (Eds), *Imagery and cognition* (pp. 133–182). New York: Springer-Verlag.

Marschark, M., Cornoldi, C., Huffman, C.J., Pé, G., & Garzari, F. (1994). Why are there *sometimes* concreteness effects in memory for prose? *Memory, 2,* 75–96.

Marschark, M., & Hunt, R.R. (1989). A reexamination of the role of imagery in learning and memory. *Journal of Experimental Psychology: Learning, Memory, and Cognition, 15,* 710–720.

Marschark, M., Richman, C.L., Yuille, J.C., & Hunt, R.R. (1987). The role of imagery in memory: On shared and distinctive information. *Psychological Bulletin, 102,* 28–41.

Marschark, M., & Surian, L. (1992). Concreteness effects in free recall: The roles of imaginal and relational processing. *Memory and Cognition, 20,* 612–620.

Marshall, J.C., Halligan, P.W., & Robertson, I.H. (1993). Contemporary theories of unilateral neglect: A critical review. In I.H. Robertson & J.C. Marshall (Eds), *Unilateral neglect: Clinical and experimental studies* (pp. 311–329). Hove, UK: Lawrence Erlbaum Associates Ltd.

Martin, C.J., Boersma, F.J., & Cox, D.L. (1965). A classification of associative strategies in paired-associate learning. *Psychonomic Science, 3,* 455–456.

Matthews, W.A. (1983). The effects of concurrent secondary tasks on the use of imagery in a free recall task. *Acta Psychologica, 53,* 231–241.

Meador, K.J., Loring, D.W., Bowers, D., & Heilman, K.M. (1987). Remote memory and neglect syndrome. *Neurology, 37,* 522–526.

Meador, K.J., Loring, D.W., Lee, G.P., Brooks, B.S., Nichols, F.T., Thompson, E.E., Thompson, W.O., & Heilman, K.M. (1989). Hemisphere asymmetry for eye gaze mechanisms. *Brain, 112,* 103–111.

Mesulam, M.-M. (1985). Attention, confusional states, and neglect. In M.-M.

Mesulam (Ed.), *Principles of behavioral neurology* (pp. 125–168). Philadelphia, PA: F.A. Davis.

Mellet, E., Tzourio, N., Denis, M., & Mazoyer, B. (1995). A positron emission tomography study of visual and mental spatial exploration. *Journal of Cognitive Neuroscience, 7,* 433–445.

Meudell, P.R. (1971). Retrieval and representations in long-term memory. *Psychonomic Science, 23,* 295–296.

Milner, B. (1966). Amnesia following operation on the temporal lobes. In C.W.M. Whitty, & O.L. Zangwill (Eds), *Amnesia* (pp. 109–133). London: Butterworths.

Milner, B. (1971). Interhemispheric differences in the localization of psychological processes in man. *British Medical Bulletin, 27,* 272–277.

Milner, B., Taylor, L., & Jones-Gotman, M. (1990). Lessons from cerebral commissurotomy: Auditory attention, haptic memory and visual images in verbal associative-learning. In C. Trevarthen (Ed.), *Brain circuits and functions of the mind: Essays in honor of Roger W. Sperry* (pp. 294–303). Cambridge, UK: Cambridge University Press.

Morris, P.E., & Stevens, R. (1974). Linking images and free recall. *Journal of Verbal Learning and Verbal Behavior, 13,* 310–315.

Moyer, R.S. (1973). Comparing objects in memory: Evidence suggesting an internal psychophysics. *Perception and Psychophysics, 13,* 180–184.

Mullen, B. (1989). *Advanced BASIC meta-analysis.* Hillsdale, NJ: Erlbaum.

Neisser, U., & Kerr, N. (1973). Spatial and mnemonic properties of visual images. *Cognitive Psychology, 5,* 138–150.

Ogden, J.A. (1985). Contralesional neglect of constructed visual images in right and left brain-damaged patients. *Neuropsychologia, 23,* 273–277.

Paivio, A. (1969). Mental imagery in associative learning and memory. *Psychological Review, 76,* 241–263.

Paivio, A. (1971). *Imagery and verbal processes.* New York: Holt, Rinehart, & Winston.

Paivio, A. (1972). A theoretical analysis of the role of imagery in learning and memory. In P.W. Sheehan (Ed.), *The function and nature of imagery* (pp. 253–279). New York: Academic Press.

Paivio, A. (1975a). Imagery and synchronic thinking. *Canadian Psychological Review, 16,* 147–163.

Paivio, A. (1975b). Perceptual comparisons through the mind's eye. *Memory and Cognition, 3,* 635–647.

Paivio, A. (1978a). Comparisons of mental clocks. *Journal of Experimental Psychology: Human Perception and Performance, 4,* 61–71.

Paivio, A. (1978b). Dual coding: Theoretical issues and empirical evidence. In J.M. Scandura & C.J. Brainerd (Eds), *Structural/process models of complex human behavior* (pp. 527–549). Alphen aan den Rijn: Sijthoff & Noordhoff.

Paivio, A. (1978c). Mental comparisons involving abstract attributes. *Memory and Cognition, 6,* 199–208.

Paivio, A. (1978d). The relationship between verbal and perceptual codes. In E.C. Carterette & M.P. Friedman (Eds), *Handbook of perception: Vol. VIII. Perceptual coding* (pp. 375–397). New York: Academic Press.

Paivio, A. (1986). *Mental representations: A dual coding approach.* New York: Oxford University Press.

Paivio, A., & Clark, J.M. (1991). Static versus dynamic imagery. In C. Cornoldi & M.A. McDaniel (Eds), *Imagery and cognition* (pp. 221–245). New York: Springer-Verlag.

Paivio, A., & Foth, D. (1970). Imaginal and verbal mediators and noun concreteness in paired-associate learning: The elusive interaction. *Journal of Verbal Learning and Verbal Behavior, 9,* 384–390.

Paivio, A., & Harshman, R.A. (1983). Factor analysis of a questionnaire on imagery and verbal habits and skills. *Canadian Journal of Psychology, 37,* 461–483.

Paivio, A., & Yuille, J.C. (1967). Mediation instructions and word attributes in paired-associate learning. *Psychonomic Science, 8,* 65–66.

Paivio, A., & Yuille, J.C. (1969). Changes in associative strategies and paired-associate learning over trials as a function of word imagery and type of learning set. *Journal of Experimental Psychology, 79,* 458–463.

Paivio, A., Yuille, J.C., & Madigan, S.A. (1968). Concreteness, imagery, and meaningfulness values for 925 nouns. *Journal of Experimental Psychology Monographs, 76*(1, Pt. 2).

Paivio, A., Yuille, J.C., & Smythe, P.C. (1966). Stimulus and response abstractness, imagery, and meaningfulness, and reported mediators in paired-associate learning. *Canadian Journal of Psychology, 20,* 362–377.

Parkin, A.J. (1984). Amnesic syndrome: A lesion-specific disorder? *Cortex, 20,* 479–508.

Parkin, A.J., & Leng, N.R.C. (1993). *Neuropsychology of the amnesic syndrome.* Hove, UK: Lawrence Erlbaum Associates Ltd.

Parrott, C.A. (1986). Validation report on the Verbalizer–Visualizer Questionnaire. *Journal of Mental Imagery, 10*(4), 39–42.

Patten, B.M. (1972). The ancient art of memory: Usefulness in treatment. *Archives of Neurology, 26,* 25–31.

Penfield, W. (1968). Engrams in the human brain. *Proceedings of the Royal Society of Medicine, 61,* 831–840.

Penfield, W., & Perot, P. (1963). The brain's record of auditory and visual experience: A final summary and discussion. *Brain, 86,* 595–696.

Perrig, W.J. (1986). Imagery and the thematic storage of prose. In D.G. Russell, D.F. Marks, & J.T.E. Richardson (Eds), *Imagery 2: Proceedings of the 2nd International Imagery Conference* (pp. 77–82). Dunedin: Human Performance Associates.

Peterson, M.A., Kihlstrom, J.F., Rose, P.M., & Glisky, M.L. (1992). Mental images can be ambiguous: Reconstruals and reference-frame reversals. *Memory and Cognition, 20,* 107–123.

Petrides, M., & Milner, B. (1982). Deficits on subject-ordered tasks after frontal- and temporal-lobe lesions in man. *Neuropsychologia, 20,* 249–262.

Pinker, S., & Kosslyn, S.M. (1978). The representation and manipulation of three-dimensional space in mental images. *Journal of Mental Imagery, 2,* 69–83.

Poltrock, S.E., & Brown, P. (1984). Individual differences in visual imagery and spatial ability. *Intelligence, 8,* 93–138.

Prigatano, G.P., Fordyce, D.J., Zeiner, H.K., Roueche, J.R., Pepping, M., & Wood, B.C. (1986). *Neuropsychological rehabilitation after brain injury.* Baltimore, MD: Johns Hopkins University Press.

Pylyshyn, Z.W. (1973). What the mind's eye tells the mind's brain: A critique of mental imagery. *Psychological Bulletin, 80,* 1–24.

Quinn, J.G., & McConnell, J. (1996). Irrelevant pictures in visual working memory. *Quarterly Journal of Experimental Psychology, 49A,* 200–215.

Quinton, A.M. (1973). *The nature of things.* London: Routledge & Kegan Paul.

Ratcliff, G. (1979). Spatial thought, mental rotation, and the right cerebral hemisphere. *Neuropsychologia, 17,* 49–54.

Reed, H.B. (1918). Associative aids: I. Their relation to learning, retention, and other associations. *Psychological Review, 25,* 128–155.

Reisberg, D., Culver, L.C., Heuer, F., & Fischman, D. (1986). Visual memory: When imagery vividness makes a difference. *Journal of Mental Imagery, 10*(4), 51–74.

Reisberg, D., & Leak, S. (1987). Visual imagery and memory for appearance: Does Clark Gable or George C. Scott have bushier eyebrows? *Canadian Journal of Psychology, 41,* 521–526.

Richardson, A. (1969). *Mental imagery.* London: Routledge & Kegan Paul.

Richardson, A. (1977a). The meaning and measurement of memory imagery. *British Journal of Psychology, 68,* 29–43.

Richardson, A. (1977b). Verbalizer–visualizer: A cognitive style dimension. *Journal of Mental Imagery, 1,* 109–125.

Richardson, A. (1978). Subject, task, and tester variables associated with initial eye movement responses. *Journal of Mental Imagery, 2,* 85–99.

Richardson, A. (1994). *Individual differences in imaging: Their measurement, origins, and consequences.* Amityville, NY: Baywood Publishing.

Richardson, J.T.E. (1975a). Concreteness and imageability. *Quarterly Journal of Experimental Psychology, 27,* 235–249.

Richardson, J.T.E. (1975b). Imagery and deep structure in the recall of English nominalizations. *British Journal of Psychology, 66,* 333–339.

Richardson, J.T.E. (1978a). Mental imagery and memory: Coding ability or coding preference? *Journal of Mental Imagery, 2,* 101–115.

Richardson, J.T.E. (1978b). Reported mediators and individual differences in mental imagery. *Memory and Cognition, 6,* 376–378.

Richardson, J.T.E. (1979a). Correlations between imagery and memory across stimuli and across subjects. *Bulletin of the Psychonomic Society, 14,* 368–370.

Richardson, J.T.E. (1979b). Mental imagery, human memory, and the effects of closed head injury. *British Journal of Social and Clinical Psychology, 18,* 319–327.

Richardson, J.T.E. (1979c). Subjects' reports in mental comparisons. *Bulletin of the Psychonomic Society, 14,* 371–372.

Richardson, J.T.E. (1980a). Concreteness, imagery, and semantic categorization. *Journal of Mental Imagery, 4,* 51–58.

Richardson, J.T.E. (1980b). *Mental imagery and human memory.* London: Macmillan.

Richardson, J.T.E. (1980c). Mental imagery and stimulus concreteness. *Journal of Mental Imagery, 4,* 87–97.

Richardson, J.T.E. (1984). The effects of closed head injury upon intrusions and confusions in free recall. *Cortex, 20,* 413–420.

Richardson, J.T.E. (1985). Integration versus decomposition in the retention of complex ideas. *Memory and Cognition, 13,* 112–127.

Richardson, J.T.E. (1987). Social class limitations on the efficacy of imagery mnemonic instructions. *British Journal of Psychology, 78,* 65–77.

Richardson, J.T.E. (1989). Performance in free recall following rupture and repair of intracranial aneurysm. *Brain and Cognition, 9,* 210–226.

Richardson, J.T.E. (1990). *Clinical and neuropsychological aspects of closed head injury.* London: Taylor & Francis.

Richardson, J.T.E. (1991). Gender differences in imagery, cognition, and memory. In R.H. Logie & M. Denis (Eds), *Mental images in human cognition* (pp. 271–303). Amsterdam: Elsevier.

Richardson, J.T.E. (1995a). The efficacy of imagery mnemonics in memory remediation. *Neuropsychologia, 33,* 1345–1357.

Richardson, J.T.E. (1995b). Gender differences in the Vividness of Visual Imagery Questionnaire: A meta-analysis. *Journal of Mental Imagery, 19*(3 & 4), 177–187.

Richardson, J.T.E., & Barry, C. (1985). The effects of minor closed head injury upon human memory: Further evidence on the role of mental imagery. *Cognitive Neuropsychology, 2,* 149–168.

Richardson, J.T.E., Cermak, L.S., Blackford, S.P., & O'Connor, M. (1987). The efficacy of imagery mnemonics following brain damage. In M.A. McDaniel & M. Pressley (Eds), *Imaginal and related mnemonic processes: Theories, individual differences and applications* (pp. 303–328). New York: Springer-Verlag.

Richardson, J.T.E., & Rossan, S. (1994). Age limitations on the efficacy of imagery mnemonic instructions. *Journal of Mental Imagery, 18,* 151–164.

Richardson, J.T.E., & Snape, W. (1984). The effects of closed head injury upon human memory: An experimental analysis. *Cognitive Neuropsychology, 1,* 213–231.

Robertson, I.H., Halligan, P.W., & Marshall, J.C. (1993). Prospects for the rehabilitation of unilateral neglect. In I.H. Robertson & J.C. Marshall (Eds), *Unilateral neglect: Clinical and experimental studies* (pp. 279–292). Hove, UK: Lawrence Erlbaum Associates Ltd.

Rohwer, W.D., Jr. (1966). Constraint, syntax and meaning in paired-associate learning. *Journal of Verbal Learning and Verbal Behavior, 5,* 541–547.

Rohwer, W.D., Jr. (1973). Elaboration and learning in childhood and adolescence. In H.W. Reese (Ed.), *Advances in child development and behavior* (Vol. 8, pp. 1–57). New York: Academic Press.

Roland, P.E., & Friberg, L. (1985). Localization of cortical areas activated by thinking. *Journal of Neurophysiology, 53,* 1219–1243.

Rollins, M. (1989). *Mental imagery: On the limits of cognitive science.* New Haven, CT: Yale University Press.

Rosenthal, R. (1966). *Experimenter effects in behavioral research.* New York: Appleton-Century-Crofts.

Runquist, W.N., & Farley, F.H. (1964). The use of mediators in the learning of verbal paired associates. *Journal of Verbal Learning and Verbal Behavior, 3,* 280–285.

Segal, S.J. (1971). Processing of the stimulus in imagery and perception. In S.J. Segal (Ed.), *Imagery: Current cognitive approaches* (pp. 69–100). New York: Academic Press.

Sergent, J. (1990). The neuropsychology of visual image generation: Data, method, and theory. *Brain and Cognition, 13,* 98–129.

Sheehan, P.W. (1966). Functional similarity of imaging to perceiving: Individual differences in vividness of imagery. *Perceptual and Motor Skills, 23,* 1011–1033.

Sheehan, P.W. (1967a). A shortened form of the Betts' Questionnaire Upon Mental Imagery. *Journal of Clinical Psychology, 23,* 386–389.

Sheehan, P.W. (1967b). Visual imagery and the organizational properties of perceived stimuli. *British Journal of Psychology, 58,* 247–252.

Sheehan, P.W. (1972). A functional analysis of the role of visual imagery in unexpected recall. In P.W. Sheehan (Ed.), *The function and nature of imagery* (pp. 149–174). New York: Academic Press.

Sheehan, P.W., & Neisser, U. (1969). Some variables affecting the vividness of imagery in recall. *British Journal of Psychology, 60*, 71–80.

Sheikh, A.A. (1977). Mental images: Ghosts of sensations? *Journal of Mental Imagery, 1*, 1–4.

Shepard, R.N. (1966). Learning and recall as organisation and search. *Journal of Verbal Learning and Verbal Behavior, 5*, 201–204.

Shepard, R.N., & Feng, C. (1972). A chronometric study of mental paper folding. *Cognitive Psychology, 3*, 228–243.

Shepard, R.N., & Metzler, J. (1971). Mental rotation of three-dimensional objects. *Science, 171*, 701–703.

Shepard, R.N., & Podgorny, P. (1978). Cognitive processes that resemble perceptual processes. In W.K. Estes (Ed.), *Handbook of learning and cognitive processes: Vol. 5. Human information processing* (pp. 189–237). Hillsdale, NJ: Erlbaum.

Shore, D.L. (1979). The effectiveness of verbal and visual imagery mnemonics in the remediation of organically based memory deficits. *Dissertation Abstracts International, 40*, 1916B.

Sitaram, N., Weingartner, H., Caine, E.D., & Gillin, J.C. (1978). Choline: Selective enhancement of serial learning and encoding of low imagery words in man. *Life Sciences, 22*, 1555–1560.

Sitaram, N., Weingartner, H., & Gillin, J.C. (1979). Choline chloride and arecoline: Effects on memory and sleep in man. In A. Barbeau, J.H. Growdon, & R.J. Wurtman (Eds), *Nutrition and the brain: Vol. 5. Choline and lecithin in brain disorders* (pp. 367–375). New York: Raven Press.

Sorabji, R. (1972). *Aristotle on memory*. London: Duckworth.

Start, K.B., & Richardson, A. (1964). Imagery and mental practice. *British Journal of Educational Psychology, 34*, 280–284.

Strack, F., & Schwarz, N. (1992). Communicative influences in standardized question situations: The case of implicit collaboration. In G.R. Semin & K. Fiedler (Eds), *Language, interaction and social cognition* (pp. 173–193). London: Sage.

Sunderland, A. (1990). The bisected image? Visual memory in patients with visual neglect. In P.J. Hampson, D.F. Marks, & J.T.E. Richardson (Eds), *Imagery: Current developments* (pp. 333–350). London: Routledge.

Tippett, L.J. (1992). The generation of visual images: A review of neuropsychological research and theory. *Psychological Bulletin, 112*, 415–432.

Toglia, M.P., & Battig, W.F. (1978). *Handbook of semantic word norms*. Hillsdale, NJ: Erlbaum.

Ungerleider, L.G., & Mishkin, M. (1982). Two cortical visual systems. In D.J. Ingle, M.A. Goodale, & R.J.W. Mansfield (Eds), *Analysis of visual behavior* (pp. 549–586). Cambridge, MA: MIT Press.

Vallar, G. (1993). The anatomical basis of spatial hemineglect in humans. In I.H. Robertson & J.C. Marshall (Eds), *Unilateral neglect: Clinical and experimental studies* (pp. 27–59). Hove, UK: Lawrence Erlbaum Associates Ltd.

Vogel, C.C., Markowitsch, H.J., Hempel, U., & Hackenberg, P. (1987). Verbal memory in brain damaged patients under different conditions of retrieval aids: A study of frontal, temporal, and diencephalic damaged subjects. *International Journal of Neuroscience, 33*, 237–256.

Voyer, D., Voyer, S., & Bryden, M.P. (1995). Magnitude of sex differences in spatial abilities: A meta-analysis and consideration of critical variables. *Psychological Bulletin, 17*, 250–270.

Warren, M.W. (1977). The effects of recall-concurrent visual-motor distraction on picture and word recall. *Memory and Cognition, 5*, 362–370.

Watson, J.B. (1914). *Behavior: An introduction to comparative psychology*. New York: Holt.

Weatherly, D.C., Ball, S.E., & Stacks, J.R. (1997). Reliance on visual imagery and its relation to mental rotation. *Perceptual and Motor Skills, 85*, 431–434.

Weingartner, H., Caine, E.D., & Ebert, M.H. (1979a). Encoding processes, learning, and recall in Huntington's disease. In T.N. Chase, N.S. Wexler, & A. Barbeau (Eds), *Advances in neurology: Vol. 23. Huntington's disease* (pp. 215–226). New York: Raven Press.

Weingartner, H., Caine, E.D., & Ebert, M. H. (1979b). Imagery, encoding, and retrieval of information from memory: Some specific encoding-retrieval changes in Huntington's disease. *Journal of Abnormal Psychology, 88*, 52–58.

White, K.D., Ashton, R., & Law, H. (1978). The measurement of imagery vividness: Effects of format and order on the Betts' Questionnaire Upon Mental Imagery. *Canadian Journal of Behavioural Science, 10*, 68–78.

Williams, J.D., Rippon, G., Stone, B.M., & Annett, J. (1995). Psychophysiological correlates of dynamic imagery. *British Journal of Psychology, 86*, 283–300.

Wittgenstein, L. (1958). *The blue and brown books*. Oxford: Blackwell.

Wolkowitz, O.M., Tinklenberg, J.R., & Weingartner, H. (1985a). A psychopharmacological perspective of cognitive functions: I. Theoretical overview and methodological considerations. *Neuropsychobiology, 14*, 88–96.

Wolkowitz, O.M., Tinklenberg, J.R., & Weingartner, H. (1985b). A psychopharmacological perspective of cognitive functions: II. Specific pharmacologic agents. *Neuropsychobiology, 14*, 133–156.

Yates, F.A. (1966). *The art of memory*. London: Routledge & Kegan Paul.

Young, A.W. (1987). Cerebral hemisphere differences and reading. In J.R. Beech & A.M. Colley (Eds), *Cognitive approaches to reading* (pp. 139–168). Chichester, UK: Wiley.

Yuille, J.C. (1973). A detailed examination of mediation in PA learning. *Memory and Cognition, 1*, 333–342.

Zaidel, D., & Sperry, R.W. (1974). Memory impairment after commissurotomy in man. *Brain, 97*, 263–272.

Author Index

Cohen, M.S., 62, 63–64, 67, 75
Cohen, W., 66
Coltheart, M., 86
Cooper, L.A., 44
Corballis, M.C., 66
Cornoldi, C., 25, 97–98, 121, 125, 129
Cox, D.L., 114
Crandall, P.H., 32
Crow, T.J., 94
Culver, L.C., 20

Davidson, R.J., 29
De Beni, R., 121, 129
Decety, J., 64
Deecke, L., 62
Della Sala, S., 69
Denis, M., vii, 26, 31, 41, 63, 127–129
De Renzi, E., 61
D'Erme, P., 72
D'Esposito, M., 31, 75
Deutsch, G., 62, 67
Di Vesta, F.J., 120
Drachman, D.A., 92

Ebert, M.H., 90–91
Edwards, J.E., 109
Ehrlichman, H., 6, 27, 28–29, 61, 86, 110, 140
Einstein, G.O., 119
Eisenberg, H.M., 62
Engle, R.W., 53
Ericsson, K.A., 112–113
Ernest, C.H., 107

Fancher, R.W., 22
Farah, M.J., 28, 29, 62, 63, 64–65, 67, 141
Farley, F.H., 114–115
Feng, C., 43–44
Finke, R.A., 24, 27, 45, 49–50, 64
Fischman, D., 20
Fordyce, D.J., 66
Foth, D., 122–123
Franklin, P.E., 79
Franks, J.J., 125
Friberg, L., 61–62
Friedland, R.P., 67, 72

Friedman, A., 47
Friendly, M., 79
Frith, C.D., 94
Fruchter, B., 39

Gade, A., 132–133
Gainotti, G., 72
Galin, D., 108
Galton, F., 10–12, 21, 22, 26, 105, 137
Garzari, F., 97–98
Gasparrini, B., 131
Gaunitz, S.C.B., 19–20
Gazzaniga, M.S., 29, 64–65, 69, 134
Gerbino, W., 25
Gillin, J.C., 93
Glisky, M.L., 25
Gloor, P., 32
Goldenberg, G., 30, 62, 69, 87, 88–89, 129, 132
Goldstein, F.C., 100
Gordon, R., 21–22
Grant, S., 51, 85
Green, K.E., 109
Grossi, D., 67, 69
Guariglia, C., 72
Guilford, J.P., 39
Gur, R.C., 19–20

Hackenberg, P., 132
Halgren, E., 32
Halligan, P.W., 68–69, 71, 72
Hammond, K.M., 63
Harris, L.J., 35–36, 37, 110
Harshman, R.A., 104, 106, 107
Hasher, L., 53
Haynes, W.O., 87
Heilman, K.M., 70
Helstrup, T., 25
Hempel, U., 132
Heuer, F., 20
Hilgard, E.R., 19–20
Hiscock, M., 39–40, 105–106, 107
Hitch, G., 51, 138
Hoc, J.M., 113
Hoffman, D., 79
Holt, R.R., 23

Holtzman, J.D., 64–65
Horowitz, S., 32
Huffman, C.J., 97–98
Hunt, R.R., 96, 98–99, 124, 125
Hyman, I.E., Jr., 25

Imamura, Y., 29
Indow, T., 24
Ingvar, D.H., 64
Intons–Peterson, M.J., 27
Isaac, A.R., 18, 20–21, 30–31

Jackson, J.H., 6
Janssen, W.H., 85, 122–123
Jones, G.V., 85
Jones, M.K., 87, 131–132, 133
Jones–Gotman, M., 88, 135

Kapur, N., 90
Kaufmann, G., 25
Kearney, E.M., 111–112, 116–117
Kerr, N., 80–81
Kihlstrom, J.F., 25
Kinsbourne, M., 108
Kintsch, W., 84–85
Kirby, J.R., 109
Kirby, K.N., 59
Kocel, K., 108
Koenig, O., 73
Kopelman, M.D., 92
Kosslyn, S.M., 6, 26, 27, 28, 31, 54–59, 63, 64–66,
    72–75, 85, 108, 138, 139, 141, 142
Kulhavy, R.W., 111, 112, 126–127
Külpe, O., 23

Lambert, A.J., 86
Law, H., 15
Leak, S., 20
LeDoux, J.E., 29
Leng, N.R.C., 132
Leplat, J., 113
Levin, H.S., 100
Levine, D.N., 28, 62, 63
Ley, R.G., 6
Lieberman, K., 51, 120–121

Linn, M.C., 36
Lister, R.G., 91
Loftus, E.F., 32
Loftus, G.R., 32
Logie, R.H., 25, 52–53, 69, 85, 108, 121, 138
Lorenz, C., 39, 40
Loring, D.W., 70
Luzzatti, C., 27, 68, 69–70

Macko, K.A., 63
Madigan, S.A., 78
Mandler, G., 124
Markowitsch, H.J., 132
Marks, D.F., 16–19, 20–21, 29–30, 106
Marquer, J., 112
Marschark, M., 95, 97–100, 124, 125, 130
Marshall, J.C., 68–69, 71, 72
Martin, C.J., 114–115
Matthews, W.A., 85
Mazoyer, B., vii, 31, 63
McConnell, J., 121
McDaniel, M.A., 111–112, 116–117, 119, 121
McDougall, S., 112, 116–117
McGeer, P.L., 93
McKelvie, S.J., 17, 18, 19, 20, 22, 36, 129
McKenna, P.J., 94
Meador, K.J., 70, 110
Mellet, E., vii, 31, 63, 75
Merrin, E.L., 108
Mesulam, M–M., 70
Metzler, J., 41–43, 62, 63–64
Meudell, P.R., 24
Milner, B., 6, 87, 88, 135
Mishkin, M., 62–63, 74
Modafferi, A., 67
Moè, A., 121
Moore, P.J., 109
Moore, W.H., 87
Morris, P.E., 123–124
Moyer, R.S., 45, 46, 49
Muckenheim, R., 79
Mullen, B., 129

Neisser, U., 16, 19, 39, 40, 80–81
Nichelli, P., 61

Stevens, R., 123–124
Stoltzfus, E.R., 53
Stone, B.M., 62
Strack, F., 16
Strayer, F.F., 109
Suess, E., 62
Sunderland, A., 68, 69, 70–71
Sunshine, P.M., 120
Surian, L., 99, 124

Tatsuno, J., 29
Taylor, L., 135
Thomson, N., 51, 85, 95
Tinklenberg, J.R., 91, 93
Tippett, L.J., 141
Togano, K., 24
Toglia, M.P., 79
Trojano, L., 67
Tzourio, N., vii, 31, 63

Uemura, K., 29
Ungerleider, L.G., 62–63, 74

Vallar, G., 67
Van Kleeck, M.H., 59
Velmans, M., 112, 116–117
Vogel, C.C., 132
Voyer, D., 36
Voyer, S., 36

Wallach, R.W., 58–59
Walter, R.D., 32

Warach, J., 63
Warren, M.W., 85
Waters, H.S., 113
Watson, J.B., 23
Weatherly, D.C., 106
Weinberger, A., 110
Weingartner, H.J., 90–91, 92, 93
Weinstein, E.A., 67, 72
Weisberg, L.L., 29
White, K.D., 15, 18
Wight, E., 51, 85
Wilkins, W., 109
Williams, J.D., 62
Williams, M., 4
Willmes, K., 62, 87, 129
Wilson, D.H., 134
Wittgenstein, L., 9
Wolkowitz, O.M., 91, 93
Wood, B.C., 66
Wundt, W., 22–23

Yates, F.A., 117
Young, A.W., 86
Yuille, J.C., 78, 96, 115, 116, 119, 121, 122, 125

Zachs, R.T., 53
Zaidel, D., 134
Zeiner, H.K., 66
Zimmerman, W.S., 39

Subject index

Acetylcholine, 91–92
After-imagery, 137
Ageing, 119–120
Ambiguous figures, 24–25
Amnesia, 132–134
Aneurysms, 89, 132–133
Anoxia, 132–133
Associative mediators, 113–115
Associative processing, 82–83
Attention window, 72–73
Attentional deficits (in unilateral neglect), 70–71
Auditory imagery, 13, 15
Availability of mediators, 116–117

Behaviourism, 23
Bilateral temporal lobectomy, 133
Bizarreness, 118–119
Brain damage, 5, 27–29, 33, 61, 62, 67–72, 87–91, 130–135
Brain mechanisms, 3–7, 140–141
Brain imaging, 4–5, 29–32
Brain stimulation, 32
"Breakfast-table questionnaire", 10–12, 105

Callosal section, *see* Commissurotomy
Cards Rotation Test, 36
Central executive processor, 51, 52
Cerebral asymmetries, 3–4, 86–88, 100, 108–110, 131, 135, 140, 414
Cerebral cortex, 3
Cerebral hemispheres, 3, 6–7, 28, 32, 61, 62, 64–67
Choline, 91, 92, 93
Cholinergic system, 91–93

Clinical neuropsychology, 5
Closed head injury, 89–90, 93–94, 100, 101, 130–131
Coding redundancy hypothesis, 83, 120
Cognitive style, 103, 104
Commissurotomised patients, *see* Split-brain patients
Commissurotomy, 5–6, 33, 134–135
Componential analysis of imagery, 6–7, 28, 58–59, 139–140
Computerised tomography (CT), 5
"Concealed" images, 81
Concreteness, 83–84
Concurrent tasks, 53–54, 85, 120–121
Construct validity, 14
Controllability of imagery, 2, 21–22
Corpus callosum, 3
Criterion validity, 14
Cued recall, 96–97, 111, 124
Cutaneous imagery, 13, 15
"Cutting a cube" task, 37, 39–40

Deep representations, 54–55
Dictionary meanings, 85
Diencephalon, 132
Differential Aptitude Test, 40
Dorsal system, 62–63, 73
Double–blind procedure, 19
Drawing a clock face, 67–69, 71
Dreaming, 27, 29, 137
Drugs, effects on memory, 91–94
Dual coding theory, 81–83, 94–95, 96, 120, 124
Dual coding versus dual processing, 98, 100, 125, 130–131, 138–139
Dual storage, 98, 138